Enjoy Your Gifted Child

Enjoy Your Gifted Child

Carol Addison Takacs

SYRACUSE UNIVERSITY PRESS

Photographs by Susan R. DeLong

Some of the material in Chapter 9 first appeared in the *Roeper Review.*

The paper used in this publication meets the minimum requirements of American National Standard for Information Sciences—Permanence of Paper for Printed Library Materials, ANSI Z39.48-1984. ∞

Library of Congress Cataloging-in-Publication Data

Takacs, Carol Addison.
  Enjoy your gifted child.

  Bibliography: p.
  Includes index.
  1. Gifted children. 2. Child rearing. I. Title.
HQ773.5.T35 1986   649'.155   85-30455
ISBN 0-8156-2356-9 (alk. paper)
ISBN 0-8156-2357-7 (pbk.)

Manufactured in the United States of America

For Cathy, Helen, and Ed

CAROL TAKACS earned her doctorate in Educational Psychology at Kent State University. She has worked extensively with gifted children and their families and teachers. As Associate Professor at Cleveland State University, she coordinates the program for preparing teachers of the gifted and talented and frequently speaks at regional and national conferences on many aspects of giftedness. Her previous publications include articles on giftedness and the broad area of teacher education. She is also the mother of three and grandmother of two.

Contents

Introduction

T HIS BOOK is written in the hope of reassuring parents of gifted and talented children and thereby increasing the enjoyment of both the parents and their children as they live fully in the present and strive courageously toward the future. Those parents who have sought my counsel have variously described their perceptions of rearing a gifted child. Some have reported the experience as awesome; others have described it as frustrating, ego-threatening, or as a chance to "shine" vicariously; as a challenge, a blessing; as a frightening responsibility; and even as a curse (Schwartz 1981). Many a mother has burst into tears as she described to me her fears of inadequacy in meeting the needs of a highly able child. A certain level of concern for the challenge is desirable and energizing, but the anxiety that seems to gnaw at the vitals of many parents is sometimes agonizing and always debilitating.

There are, of course, large numbers of parents who are meeting the challenge in positive and joyful ways. One of the goals of this book will be a sharing of the attitudes and activities which have contributed to family harmony and individual growth. The attitude most likely to engender productive and happy parent-child relationships combines both challenge and blessing with a seasoning of humor.

Throughout this book, the work of leading figures in human development will be explored and brought to bear on those aspects of giftedness which can bring both concern and pleasure to child-rearing experiences. Interviews with parents and children will be used as illustrative examples.

Through both extensive reading and years of experience, I have come to an awareness that parents who become members of associations for gifted children seem to have more problems with their youngsters than do parents of equally bright youngsters who choose not to publicly and formally identify themselves or their children as gifted. Since much of my own professional activity has related to such groups at local, state, and national levels, it may be that the tribulations of parents are more frequently brought home to me than are the triumphs of which I am also aware. After a recent meeting with a large group of parents in which school problems were the major focus, one father, whose quizzical response had been evident throughout the session, approached me with his wife. They said with genuine concern, "Our daughter doesn't have any of those symptoms. Does that mean she isn't gifted?"

As we respond to the problems that do exist, let us not lose sight of the many well-adjusted, thriving gifted and talented youngsters who constitute the majority of our highly able children. To do otherwise would be to nurture the stereotype of unhappy, solitary, genius which has contributed so much to the negative perception of "giftedness" in our society and which adds to the anxiety of parents.

It has been said often but must be said again and emphasized strongly. Gifted children are first and foremost children. (I have often suggested that such an organization as NAGC—National Organization for Gifted Children—change its title to NACG—National Association for Children who are Gifted.)

These children have more commonalities with the whole of the human race than they have differences from it. When we as parents, teachers, or peers respond to those few unique characteristics out of all balance with the many other aspects of personhood, we do our gifted youngsters a tremendous injustice. This may be the key to most of the tensions and difficulties which arise in the families of gifted and talented children. Significant numbers of adolescents who are both gifted and have emotional problems report their perception that their parents only valued them for their "gifts"—that parents never saw them as persons or valued anything about them other than that special area of excellence. Of course, these troubled youngsters represent the extremes in the examples of parent-child miscommunication, but, to the extent that the brilliant glow of the child's gift blinds us to the child's personhood, we may endanger the healthy development of the concept of self.

Many miscommunications that parents convey to their children are unfelt and unintended. This book is intended to increase understanding of human behavior and children's needs in the family setting and, through heightened sensitivity, to prevent pain and promote joy.

One of the best-known writers on personality development is Abraham Maslow (1954) and he speaks of various levels at which human beings actually function.

At the least comfortable level, one sees the person *surviving*. Both physical and emotional energies are completely tied up in staying alive and hanging on to reality. One rung higher on the ladder of personal adjustment is the individual *defending*. Some foothold of physical and emotional security has been obtained, but its possession is continually threatened and the maintenance of this small island of security occupies all of the individual's energies. At a more satisfactory level is the person ·who is *coping*. Physical and emotional emergies are in balance with the demands of the environment and a considerable degree of psychological security has been achieved. There is sufficient energy for productive action. At the most desirable level of functioning one finds the fortunate person who is *flourishing*. Secure in a sense of effective self in a responsive environment, such an individual has a wealth of physical and psychological energy which can be devoted to the enrichment and enjoyment of life both for self and for others.

These levels of functioning also apply to family structures and relationships. It is with the hope that more families will flourish in the enjoyment of their richness that this book is offered.

This book is organized into the following four sections: Part I focuses on the *Discovery* of the special talents, by the parents, by the child, and by brothers and sisters. Part II emphasizes *Nurturing* the child during vital formative years. Part III, *Cherishing*, explores the enriching support the parents can provide which enables the child to flourish. Part IV looks forward to *Sharing* the maturing person as the child takes his or her place in school and community. This last step also involves that most difficult task for parents, letting go.

PART I

Discovery

1

Multidimensionality of Giftedness

WHAT IS IT about the very young child which leads parents to suspect that their child is gifted and then to seek expert verification of their earliest discovering? The most frequently noted facet is early talking and extensive vocabulary. Also mentioned often are extraordinary alertness (she notices everything), insatiable curiosity (there's nothing he won't get into), and an excellent memory (she can "read" her storybooks after hearing them twice).

While these precocious behaviors are usually precursors of superior intellectual performance, not all gifted and talented children show parents these or similar early flashes of brilliance. It will be helpful, at the outset, to describe the most generally observed characteristics shared by many children who are gifted. Giftedness is multidimensional, and the professional community has largely accepted the definition set forth by the U.S. Office of Education (Marland 1977). Its report states that a gifted student can be identified by professionally qualified persons as one with outstanding abilities, a potential for high performance and demonstrated achievement in any one of six areas, including general intellectual ability, creative or productive thinking, specific academic aptitude, leadership ability, visual and performing arts ability, and psychomotor abilities. Although the last-named criterion has been dropped as an official category for federal funding, it is still one of the most widely recognized categories of talent, the gifted athlete.

It seemed superfluous to provide federal aid in an area which already enjoys widespread partisanship and financial bounty from

3

pee-wee league through NFL and NBA. This is one area of excellence in America in which the label of gifted has shed the stigma of elitism. Some parents can and do boast openly of an offspring's athletic prowess while others are secretive and understandably protective about their offspring's intellectual prowess. It is socially acceptable to be strongest and fastest, but small are the circles in which it is comfortable to be smartest. The Football Hall of Fame is a national shrine, while Mensa is practically a secret society.

The identifying characteristics of giftedness can be described in three overlapping categories—advanced cognitive development, psychosocial, and physical performance.

COGNITIVE

In the area of advanced cognitive development, the following are usually observed.

There is *broad perceptual sensitivity*, with children taking in everything in the environment. They have the ability to attend to several things at one time. In his extensive research with preschoolers, Burton White (1971) found that the best predictor of academic success at age six was the ability of some three-year-olds to attend simultaneously to more than one event in their surroundings.

They have *tremendous curiosity* about how things work, why things are, what if conditions were changed? They need to explore the environment actively and to experiment with it. All children are curious, but the gifted child often will not permit exploration to be curtailed. When one considers these propensities in the light of Jean Piaget's (1952) model of human cognitive functioning it is easy to see this information processing function of the mind as analogous to the nutrient processing function of the body. It is as natural for the brain to learn as for the lungs to breathe. The individual's craving for novelty and mental stimulation is as basic a need as that of hunger or thirst. In fact, the state of being that is most intolerable to a human organism is that of boredom! If you are deeply interested in something, you forget hunger and fatigue, you postpone material gratification. On the other hand, if you are bored you will seek out any source of stimulation, including reading cereal boxes or the wrappers on bathroom tissue. What brain researchers are beginning to tell us about the biochemical and electrical activity of the brain suggests that these activities are speeded up in our gifted and talented children. Their brains have immense appetites, accompanied by gargantuan digestive powers. But, as we shall see, even they sometimes bite off more than they can chew. (The mind's eye may, on occasion, be bigger than the mind's digestive capability.)

Apparent in young gifted children is the *ability to see relationships* and to make inferences about causality and functions. They particularly like patterns and systems, often enjoy fantasizing alternative systems. This ability underlies many of the intuitive leaps or "step-skipping" common to exceptionally bright youngsters. Not only do their synapses seem to snap faster, their networks seem to have more connections. That "what if?" switch seems to be always open. They enjoy the patterns most when they discover them on their own and often perceive patterns that no one noticed before.

They are usually blessed with *excellent memory* nourished by early language and symbolic abilities. These combined strengths enable children to classify and categorize information and experiences, providing mental storage strategies which greatly enhance retrieval. They make up their own mnemonic devices just for fun. Evidence for their pleasure in classifying and categorizing can be found in a favorite hobby of gifted children—collections. Much of their enjoyment involves the ordering, organizing, and reordering of the specimens in the collection. A tidy permanent display is not the goal.

The attribute which earliest and most often draws the attention of others to the gifted child is an *extensive vocabulary* accompanied by sophisticated syntactic structures. They use big words and put together complex sentences and ask articulate, sometimes embarrassing, questions often in public places. Young gifted children love to read dictionaries and encyclopedias but lack the experiential referents of more mature speakers. They often make up words to suit idiosyncratic meanings and imaginary events. They love to play with language.

Gifted children have a much higher than average ability to *tolerate cognitive ambiguity* and resist early closure. They enjoy complex and open-ended tasks and hate to be told the answer. Herein lies the germ of future conflict in the classroom. (Most elementary teachers have a high need for closure, already know the answers to the questions they ask, and usually wait less than five seconds for a pupil to respond before supplying the answers.)

Some have *advanced mathematical skills* in both computation and reasoning. These interests may suppress reading precocity. One youngster of my acquaintance was mentally multiplying three digit numbers by three digit numbers (376 × 984) at age five faster than my 26-year-old brain could do it assisted by pencil and paper, but he showed no interest in reading and resisted stubbornly the best efforts of his early teachers. Phillip's nursery school expulsion led to psychological testing at age four which showed his I.Q. to be in the 200 + range. Of course he could have read. He simply did not want to.

Notable also is an *extended concentration span* with high task persistence in areas of interest. This is accompanied by intensity of task involvement. Completion of an engineering project in the sandbox or at the water table is much more important than snack time or an impending rain shower. Because they are so young, these children lack the foresight and prudence which come only through experience and so they often undertake more than can reasonably be accomplished. They need adult understanding and moderating guidance, but they should try sometimes and fail and then come back to try again.

PSYCHOSOCIAL

In the realm of psychosocial development, an area in which Erikson (1950) and Kohlberg (1969) have given us important insights, the following personal and emotional characteristics are frequently evident in gifted and talented children.

A strong *sense of justice,* what is fair or unfair, appears very early. Illustrative of this is the story one mother shared with me about her older son's first Sunday school experience. Hardy came home insisting angrily that, "God is not fair!" The lesson that day had been a Bible story about Noah's Ark, with its emphasis on both the destructive flood and the animals saved only two-by-two. Three-year-old Hardy said, "God told the people what they were supposed to do and what would happen if they were bad. So it was all right for them to be drowned. But he didn't tell the animals, he never warned them, so they shouldn't have to die—God is not fair!"

The *personal value systems* of young gifted children have a broad compass. They perceive injustices in the larger society, set high standards for self and others, and respond to truth, justice, harmony, and nature. The far-ranging scope of television brings evidence of distant problems into our living rooms and young gifted viewers expect, sometimes demand, that parents take direct action in response to famine in Africa, refugees from Southeast Asia, baby seals in the Arctic, and they will empty their own piggy-banks in such causes.

Gifted children revel in a *vivid imagination.* During the years between two and five before concrete realism has usually taken precedence in mental operations, all children fail to make "rational" distinctions between fact and fantasy. Gifted children are so adept at embellishing and extending their fantasies verbally and they enter so intensively into them that parents and teachers occasionally get overly concerned about the child's ability to distinguish truth from fiction. This vivid imagination generates imaginary friends, desired siblings, a rich and rewarding fantasy life. As they grow older, many are able to retain a playfulness in work, inventiveness, and creativity, traits which have contributed so much to human progress on the material level as well as the aesthetic quality of human life.

One of the most important traits for the gifted individual in terms of personal adjustment is a *great sense of humor.* They love incongruities, puns, and pranks, and they often see things as funny when peers do not. Humor can be a saving grace and a healthy cushion shielding the sensitive psyche from the buffets of less-perceptive others in many interactive situations. This resilient sense of humor which can bring such zest to family life can also evoke less positive responses from some teachers, who may not always "get the joke" or appreciate it when they do. Few of us are so secure in our self-concepts that we can join whole-heartedly in the laughter when the joke is on us.

Young gifted children are *easily frustrated,* as are most preschool children. They continually attempt tasks they can not yet master, and that attempt is developmentally appropriate. However, because gifted children are successful beyond their years in some of the tasks they attempt, this may lead parents (and retroactively the children themselves) to expect similar easy mastery in all areas. We call these over-generalized adult expectations the "halo-effect" and caution against it all those who work with gifted youngsters at any stage of development. In the early years, gifted children are like others their age in their emotional dependence, their impatience, their lack of emotional balance. They are often more intense in their expressions of these traits because they have superior powers of communication. These precocious verbal abilities can lead to adult misperceptions of a young child's emotional maturity level and this compounds the problem.

Research shows that the fears of young children are usually not realistic. It is difficult for the parents of city-bred six-year-olds to comprehend that their children are more fearful of lions and tigers and other large wild animals than they are of automobiles or trucks which they are much more likely to encounter. The tremendous popularity of Maurice Sendak's *Where the Wild Things Are* is notable evidence of this. Gifted children often have *exaggerated fears* because they are able to imagine so many more dire possibilities. Also, they are exceptionally sensitive to the nonverbal signs of those about them and are highly vulnerable to unspoken tensions in their surroundings.

One giant in the study of gifted individuals (Gowan 1972) postulates extrasensory perception as among the superior abilities possessed by that population. Several instances of ESP interaction have been described to me in some detail by teachers of elementary gifted classes. One boy thought he was "crazy," "insane," because of his thought reading and prevision of subsequent events. Understandably, the teacher was also shaken by his unburdening. We actually know so little about the biochemistry or electrical energy of the brain that it would be frivolous to dismiss out-of-hand the possibilities of telepathy or clairvoyance even though they are presently outer-fringe notions to the majority of empirical scientists. Such experiences do appear with relative frequency in highly gifted youngsters and should be met with open-mindedness rather than an incredulity which may intensify their fears of personal abnormality. They need reassurance, not ridicule. Perhaps they "see more clearly" what less sensitive mortals "see in the glass darkly."

In the preschool years, gifted children are *developmentally egocentric* in the interpretations of experience, just as their less able age peers are. Egocentricity is a term Piaget gave us which helps us to understand some of the qualitative differences between preschoolers' intuitive, animistic view of the world and the older child's more rational, concrete reality-oriented view. Egocentric does not mean selfish in its common pejorative connotation. It does mean projecting one's own cognitive awareness and emotional response to an event onto the minds and hearts of all others present at the event. We call it colloquially, "being one-way," not being receptive to the experiences and attitudes of others, and we find it reprehensible in adults. So it is, but it is normal in preschool children, no matter how bright. As the child's developing mind begins to be conscious of its own functioning, thinking about thinking, or metacognition as the experts now call it, the child believes that the awareness of events in his or her own head is identical to the simultaneous conscious awareness in the heads of all others present. In other words, all who share in an experience perceive it and interpret it in exactly the same way (the way I see it). Adults know, intellectually, that this is not true, but we never totally outgrow our three-to-five-year-old egocentricity and often find it hard to value the differing point of view of another, especially when it is based on parallel experiences.

When childish egocentricity is combined with the sensitivity and impatience with ineptitude which are common to gifted children, peer adjustment problems can and often do result. The most frequently grasped-at remedy, that of "talking it out" with the precociously verbal four-year-old who manipulates adults with five-syllable words, will not get at the root of the difficulty which is the normal, developmental egocentricity of the child. This is sometimes referred to as adultizing the child. She cannot yet understand that others experience the world and its daily events quite differently than she does. In later chapters some developmentally appropriate strategies will be suggested.

It is not uncommon, then, for gifted children to encounter low social acceptance from age peers and to suffer as a consequence from *negative self-concepts*. It is understandably difficult for many parents and professionals to accept the research evidence that a large proportion of our most able youngsters have negative feelings, feelings of inadequacy, about themselves (Leaverton and Herzog 1979). Some social activities with similarly gifted age peers from the most tender years will prove most beneficial in promoting a healthy self-concept and a needed sense of full membership in the human race. Supportive families, with parents, brothers, and sisters sharing many activities, also foster positive feelings about self. It is very sad that parents of gifted children have significantly fewer offspring than do families on the average.

One mother said to me, "When we realized early that George was gifted, we decided right then not to have any more children so that we could devote all our time and resources to him. He goes everywhere with us and participates in everything we do." Possibly the most enjoyable and humanizing resource they might have given him was brothers or sisters. Siblings would at least have spread out the hot-house focus of the undiluted attention of two doting and expectant adults. In their book *Cradles of Eminence* (1962), Goertzels and Goertzels state that such a family background does produce some high-performance adults, whose personal histories, however, reflect a life-long inability to achieve intimacy with another person. For a fuller understanding of how this may take place, Erikson's stages of psychosocial development will be discussed in Chapter 7.

PHYSICAL

There are two competing stereotypes relative to the physical characteristics of gifted children. The first is of the skinny, undersized, pale, bespectacled bookworm (*Saturday Review* 1979). The other is that promulgated by Terman's monumental *Studies of Genius* (1925), which tells us that gifted children are taller, sturdier, healthier, and more attractive than their unexceptional age peers. While the latter is preferable to the former, neither is quite true. The children Terman studied were middle- and upper-class whites who, as a population group, are taller, sturdier, healthier, better nourished, and some say more attractive than other groups in the American population. As we widen the scope of identification processes to accommodate the multidimensionality of giftedness and to balance for the social class and cultural bias of standardized test instruments, we find that the physical characteristics of gifted children are as varied as are all children. It is not valid to make stereotypic generalizations about the height, weight, health, or appearance of gifted children. They are excitingly diverse.

There is one physiological difference that has been recorded in the life styles of productive adults and which is complained of by parents of very young gifted children. They have exceedingly *high energy levels* and often need less than expected amounts of sleep. Parents wonder what they are doing wrong when the pediatrician has told them that their newborn will sleep 20 hours out of 24 and it seems to the exhausted parents that it's more like 4 out of 24! Of course, this is an exaggeration but the majority of parents interviewed indicate that their gifted children slept less than normal as infants, gave up naps much too early to suit mothers and nursery school teachers, and still fight bedtime fiercely. This is so frequently reported that one suspects there is a genetic metabolic basis for the behavior. A trait that can be conducive to high productivity in adults is challenging to parents in childhood.

Fine motor coordination, manual dexterity, and eye-hand coordination are more closely age-related and usually not as advanced as cognition. Young hands need training and many practice opportunities. Cutting and pasting can be more difficult than adding and subtracting, writing much harder than reading or speaking. This unevenness in comparison to development norms often leads to frustration and an increase in dependency behaviors. It also requires careful individualization in early programming for gifted children in order to prevent life-long distaste for necessary basic skills.

One professional educator recently described his five-year-old gifted son as highly verbal and intellectually precocious but slow in psychomotor skills. My questioning established that his psychomotor development was normal for his age, and, while it might be characterized as less advanced than his cognitive skills, it certainly was not slow. This is just one example of the possibly negative impact of the halo effect, even with parents or teachers well trained in child development.

The preceding paragraphs provide a brief description of a few of the many facets of giftedness. These are the ones most frequently reported by researchers and parents as descriptive of the gifted children they know. Each individual child will have unique facets which are not mentioned here but which contribute a special beauty. There is not room to describe all those possibilities, but they are equally vital components in the discovery and enjoyment of each of our youngsters.

2

Discovery by Parents

A s would be expected, parents are most often the first to notice giftedness in a child, although this is not inevitable. Gifted children can be so different from each other and express their gifts in so many ways that their special abilities are not always evident to parents.

Absence of early identification is noted most often in the case of first or only children where the parents lack a basis for comparison. Such parents often report, "I just thought that was how all babies acted."

In families where all the children are gifted, parents sometimes tend to view them as "just regular kids" and not be aware in the early years that their children have superior intelligence. It happens too that working-class parents who stopped their own education early sometimes fail to notice signs of precocious development in their children and are surprised when the school authorities inform them that their son or daughter has been tested and found eligible for the gifted program in grade four.

It can happen that such identification is resisted. Parents of gifted children are of course susceptible to the attitudes and values of the larger society. The over application of democratic values and glorification of the common person have largely contributed to historic and present anti-intellectualism in America (Hofstader 1963).

Many parents will say, "I don't want my child to be gifted, just let him be a normal, well-adjusted, happy child!" Or, when asked about their own feelings about raising a gifted child, report that everything was fine until the school attached the label and told them the child was gifted. The child was the same child, but the parents' perception of the child changed and they often became more anxious about their responsibilities, which can permit tension to drive joy out of the family relationship. There is also the possibility that the child's perception of self is altered by the labeling but that question will be taken up in Chapter 7.

In attempting to understand and respond to parental anxiety, one is struck by the implications of the opening quote in the preceding paragraph. Do thinking adults honestly believe that being gifted means to be abnormal, maladjusted, and unhappy? Sadly, those are widespread negative stereotypes of giftedness which even parents sometimes share. Such attitudes can seriously hamper the normal, happy adjustment of a child; the stereotypes need to be confronted and eradicated. Denying or ignoring the unique abilities of a child because of social mores will definitely not contribute to that child's adjustment or happiness.

The ideal parental response of glad acceptance falls in the happy middle ground between ignoring and exploiting the child's gifts.

Returning to the initial statement that the primary discoverers of gifted children are parents, here are those early behaviors most often reported in the literature (Vail 1979; Martinsen 1974) and my own parent interviews. While early talking, big words, and early reading or computing are usually cited by parents, intense curiosity ("She asks a million questions about everything") and retentive memory ("He can recall things in such detail") are frequently mentioned. More importance should be attached to the latter traits, as well as quick understanding ("I only have to tell her once"), imagination ("He has imaginary playmates" or "She tells me the most fantastic tales") rather than to specific achievements like counting or reading. "Sesame Street," educational toys, and parental or big sister tutoring all can promote the latter skills in children who may not be mentally precocious. Centuries ago, Plato advised those who would train the leaders of the future, "select those tenacious of memory and hard to deceive." Maybe the old skill game of Concentration (now available for the home computer) would be a valid screening measure.

In more recent times, Terman and Miles (1936) noted what may be a middle-class white American phenomenon. For his sample of 1,200 gifted youngsters, three-fourths of the parents noticed intellectual superiority in their daughters before age 3½, but in boys a little later. One might speculate about the weight given to early talking and large vocabulary and the greater volume of talking that mothers traditionally do with little girls, conversing less with their sons (Moss 1967).

It should be noted here that, significant as the Terman study has been for understanding giftedness, it is based almost entirely on a middle- and upper-middle-class white population. Other cultural patterns in child rearing emphasize and reinforce differing behaviors, and the early identification characteristics derived from his writing probably do not provide adequate parallels for all cultures. In particular, the findings of physical superiority in height, weight, and health to national norms for the entire child population of the country at that time, while they counteract the negative image of the puny, sickly bookworm, actually reflect an over-all middle-class superiority to national norms in physical development.

Gifted children are as diverse in their stature, weight, and health as are all children, and their physiological development is not likely to be advanced over age mates in the way that cognitive growth is.

Given a broad commonality of quick understanding, great curiosity, good memory, imagination, and insight, gifted children manifest their myriad gifts in quite different ways, sometimes choosing not to manifest them at all. Not all exceptionally bright children talk early even when the capability is there. One young woman of my acquaintance said no words until she was three, and simply began to speak at that time in complete sentences. She says she felt no need to talk (in the shadow of her older brother). Throughout the first years of school she also refused to talk because the teachers did not address her by the name she preferred. Neither mother nor teacher recognized the prodigious abilities she chose not to manifest. The young woman went on to achieve a C average in college, earning As in science and math, which she liked, and Fs in the subjects she did not. She now enjoys a rewarding international career in the computer field, based on a B.S. degree in math and an enormous amount of expertise.

It has been my personal experience in primary classrooms that little boys from poor black families are more verbal than little girls from similar families, reversing the language advantage predicted for females in early school years. There is a possible explanation in differing child-mother interactions in different cultures. Similar experiences have led others (Baldwin 1978; Frasier 1985) to question the broadly accepted criteria in identification of young gifted children and to consider carefully the differing environments in which individual children develop.

Mention of teachers and the personal importance attached to the use of names brings to mind a peerless illustration of the sensitivity and logic to be found in the young gifted child.

Hardy's mother sent him off to kindergarten with warm expectations for his enjoyment of the new experiences. She was therefore somewhat surprised and a little apprehensive to receive a call from Hardy's teacher a bare three weeks later. The teacher opened the conversation by describing her own annual procedure for breaking her pupils of the persistent tendency to call her "Teacher." She announced on Day One and continually reminded her little charges that her name was "Mrs. Johnson," and that she was not to be addressed as, "Teacher." This had always effectively stopped the undesirable practice in the past. It seems that, despite constant admonitions, Hardy had continued to call out, "Teacher," when he needed her attention, until that morning when, in exasperation, she had said sharply, "Young man, now how many times have I told you not to call me 'Teacher.' My name is Mrs. Johnson!" To which Hardy then responded quietly, "I know. I'm sorry, but every time you call me 'Young Man' I seem to forget." Happily, the teacher was also sensitive and had telephoned not to scold but to share the experience with Hardy's mother and to indicate her own heightened awareness of the need to respect the dignity of children, who are also entitled to be addressed by their preferred names.

Parental response to the challenge of parenthood is also extremely diverse as was underscored by the contrasting responses of two fellow doctoral students in educational psychology. When asked informally to relate a peak experience (Maslow 1954) which stood out in their memories, the first young man answered quickly with a beaming smile, "Without a doubt, the moment I held my firstborn son in my arms in the hospital nursery!" His companion, also a recent father, simply gasped, "Oh, no," he said, "that was a truly fearful moment for me, as I held him and thought about all that he would need and what I wanted to do for him in the future." It would appear that the first would find much more joy than anxiety in his familial responsibilities. It is to be hoped that the

second gained security from experience. Both are now school psychologists.

The discovery that one's child is gifted should result in pleasurable anticipation and zest for the challenge rather than a debilitating anxiety that constricts the spontaneity of the most
important relationship for individual development, that of parent
and child. This is not to belittle the challenge of nurturing a
youngster who sleeps less, explores more, perceives more, and
understands more, not to mention says more, but to hearten the
readers to relish the task.

3

Discovery by the Child

T HE WAY in which the child discovers his or her own giftedness
is a matter of great interest to parents. Mothers and fathers
are concerned about appropriate responses to a child's first inkling
of uniqueness. With some gifted children who have extensive contact with brothers and sisters and same-age playmates, awareness
of differentness may come early. For many others, the consciousness of special abilities first surfaces as a result of school
entry and the enforced comparisons brought about in classrooms.

What parents seek is a healthy self-perception and some understanding on the child's part that the abilities and sensitivities of
other children and adults may be at different levels or in different
areas from their own. The social and emotional consequence of
these differences are much more delicate than the cognitive or
mental understanding.

It is one thing to know in your mind but a very different thing
to feel it in your gut. A major contribution to a gifted child's
healthy self-perception is a sense of commonality with all persons
in basic membership in human society and a beginning appreciation of the wide variety of characteristics which are valued by
individuals in that society. In most ways the child is like all children, but in a few special ways the child is unique.

The task parents face is one of finding the appropriate occasions, words, and examples to communicate these very large ideas
to very young children. The precocity of these children brings
about the need for such communication quite early. This communication takes place not only verbally, but it is also expressed power-

fully in the behaviors and attitudes of parents and others as they respond to the growing child.

Here it should be said that the advanced verbal skills of many gifted children contribute to an overdependence on the part of parents and teachers on talking and explaining, the interchange of words. This can lead to a veneer of apparent understanding that may well be contradicted in day-to-day activities.

The entire range of experiences communicates to a child's understanding. Words are not the dominant channel for young children. There should be a congruence between parental discussions and parental behaviors that will reinforce the child's sense of what is valued and what is expected and provide a secure base for developing self-awareness.

How does one's image of self develop? Psychologists (Mussen 1970) tell us that it is a distillation of the response that people and our environment make to us. The exploring child learns from experience what she can or cannot accomplish in physical settings, and the people in her environment show her in many ways how valuable those accomplishments are. An individual's behavior is very much determined by what pays off. The rewards may be extrinsic or intrinsic, primary or secondary, material or spiritual, short-term or long-term according to the models of various psychological theorists. A person of any age continues and increases behaviors which result in desired outcomes and ceases those behaviors which do not.

For the young child, the desired outcomes center around mastery of manipulation and meaning in the physical environment and the attention and caring of parents, the significant others in that environment. It is comparatively easy for parents to observe, guide, and tutor the mastery of the physical environment, even when the "why" questions seem endless and home appliances are dismantled by probing little fingers. It is more challenging to balance parental expression of caring and pleasure in order to prevent an unwitting overemphasis on a particular area of outstanding competence, to the possible detriment of the child's perception of what parents truly value.

Parents are often troubled by what they report as a gifted child's inborn need to excel, to be the best, to be perfect. The behaviors and temperament which accompany the drive for perfection are rightly seen by parents as potentially painful for the child, often leading to feelings of frustration, as well as being unappealing to others.

It should be noted here that Benjamin Bloom (1982), who has headed a study of preeminent young achievers in the fields of swimming, tennis, music, math, sculpture, and neurology, finds this drive to excel one of the early "markers" of future recognition. He and his assistants describe in some detail how this drive seems to be engendered and nurtured by the family in a parental plan for making the most of a child's ability and promoting future stardom. The published reports of this study (Bloom and Sosniak 1981) would be of great interest to parents as they introspect about their value systems and their hopes for a child's future.

One statement of particular interest to this writer was that the parents of the selected young achievers sometimes reported that other siblings had showed equal or greater early ability but never developed the drive for excellence that characterized the starring child. It would seem a fascinating corollary avenue of investigation to also interview those brothers and sisters about their early perceptions and experiences and to compare their life adjustment with that of the more successful performers.

Those who are raising young gifted children need to look to their own patterns of response to their children for much of the strength of the need to excel in their children. To what aspects of the child's behavior do the parents respond most intensely and regularly? What brings the quickest smile, approving glance, the attentive turn of the head? What activities are described in tones of loving pride in telephone conversations that are usually overheard and well understood by the impressionable youngster? What happenings are fondly related to Dad or Grandma?

And what well-meant, but pernicious, carrying-on do doting grandparents permit themselves! Grandparents' license to spoil is legendary, but they can unwittingly do really off-base things to little ones. Can you see proud Grandpa at a family restaurant outing, proclaiming over the blond curly head of the three-year-old cuddled happily on his lap, "Janet will read the menu for us. Now listen everybody, Janet is going to tell us what it says we can have to eat. Read it now for all of us, Honey. Go ahead." And all eyes turn expectantly to Janet, family members, waiters, other customers. The performance ensues; the folks are impressed; the oohs and aahs are heard, and Janet just may be perceiving that reading is what people like best about her. Her sand castles, dough messes, self-dressing, toy-storing, mother-helping or patient turn-waiting do not evoke such extravagant praise and, thus, cannot be as worthwhile.

This is certainly not to say that the expressions of talents and gifts in such children are to be ignored, but rather that they not be exploited out of proportion to other desirable capabilities and traits.

When attention and reinforcement for the unique gift do get far out of balance, the resulting influence on the self-image of the child can be quite other than what proud parents intend. Teenaged gifted youngsters suffering from emotional disturbances almost uniformly tell counselors, in retrospect, that their parents "never saw me as a person. They only saw my achievement. They don't even know me." Too often, it seems, the shining gift has blinded parents to the child. It has happened to gifted musicians and athletes as well as intellectually superior youngsters. Bloom suggests that some parents may actually be seeking out signs of a particular gift and over-evaluating those signs. Parents who enjoy a special talent or interest themselves tend to overemphasize this area with their children and to expect a similar ability and involvement in the child. Personality factors or family constellations may lead different children in the same family to react either negatively or positively to these parental priorities.

In a revealing book by one of the Quiz Kids of the 1940s, a former child prodigy discusses the adult lives of fellow contestants (R. D. Feldman 1982). The lasting impact of early adulation is movingly described in those pages.

Parents can profitably introspect and interact in examination and definition of their own human and social values. What are the important things in life? What do they want for the child? All would agree that health and happiness top the list, including mental as well as physical health. In light of these universal priorities, what virtues are they attending to, what areas of weakness are being strengthened in their hourly, daily family living? What rewards are given for helpfulness, patience, perseverance, responsibility, generosity of spirit, optimism, bravery, honesty, as these developing traits are expressed in little actions. Surely, when one thinks about it, these are jewels as precious as IQ or perfect pitch. The positive outcome for parents of thinking about these matters should be a more desirable balance in what parents give attention to, smile about, praise, and fondly describe in a child's behavior. For such parental responses are the precious rewards, the payoff for the child, and the ultimate shapers of the child's self-concept and self-esteem.

Parents should ask, "What do I see and value in this child, and how do I let him know what I value?" Then the mirrors of caregiver response in which the child sees himself defined should more accurately reflect the many-faceted image of a child who is gifted, a whole wonderful person in contrast to the fun-house mirror distortions of a blown-out-of-proportion isolated talent.

In presenting the worst-case example, an author risks non-involvement on the part of the audience. Reading an extreme example, the mother or father may say, "Oh, we're never like that, but some people we know are." Fortunately, the extreme cases are infrequent, but there is a whole continuum of lack of proportion in rewarding certain behaviors. Parents should be vigilant and honest with themselves in preventing any unhealthy imbalance in the family support and reinforcement system for their gifted children.

Beyond warning about what parents should avoid as they play their central role in the child's discovery of her own giftedness, what direct action should parents take as a child begins to seek information about the difference she may experience? What can an adult say honestly, in a form that the child will understand? What are the experiences that can give rise to the child's questions? What are some guidelines for parental explanations to young children?

The following possibly apocryphal anecdote serves well as a rule of thumb for parental explanations. One day, five-year-old Brian popped in from afternoon kindergarten and asked his mother to tell him something about Mars. "Why don't you ask your father when he gets home?" she responded. "After all, he's an astronomer." To which Brian replied, "Yes, but I really don't want to know all that much." Children in that family and students in this writer's classes have been taught now to say "Mars" whenever the response to a question threatens to provide all that much more than the asker really wanted to know.

Awareness of the experiences which have resulted in a child's concern can also guide parental choice about what to say. It happens that a gifted child is much quicker or better at a given task than a brother or sister, even an older one. The younger is impatient and the older is frustrated. Indicate to the gifted child that each individual learns different things at different rates and that he is fortunate to be a very fast learner in a particular area (or areas) but that love and kindness should help him also to learn patience with others who can not learn so rapidly. Tell him that you will try to help him find opportunities to share his special abilities with others who match his pace in that skill. It is important that the child understand something about the uniqueness of his ability but also that some others share that unique ability to a similar degree. He is different from some, but also like others. The pleasures he should take in his own special qualities need to be balanced by an appreciation of the different but also special qualities of siblings and playmates.

The gifted child may be more intellectually able than her readily available neighborhood playmates and will often tend either to dominate them or be bored by them. It should be explained to her that her ability to understand, to figure things out, to put words together, progresses more rapidly than theirs and that she needs to give them more time to work things through for themselves. One developmentally suitable strategy is role play. Since the three-to-five-year-old child is often not able to take the point of view of another but naturally learns from trying on various roles, create with her a situation in which you take the role of the child of superior talents and give her incomplete directions, tell her answers before she has an opportunity to figure out for herself and scold her for incorrect or slow responses.

Such interactions seldom occur for highly gifted youngsters in real life, and they lack opportunities to learn in developmentally appropriate ways just how their behaviors affect others. Just telling them to "put yourself in her shoes," or asking after an unpleasant experience, "How would you feel if Kim did that to you?" are not always useful requests when directed to preschool youngsters. Their normal egocentrism can block such vicarious sensibilities and requires caring adults to seek alternate strategies for helping a young child to truly understand.

Unless accompanied by vivid parallel examples which the child herself has recently experienced, such suggestions sometimes fail to evoke the desired empathetic response in preschool youngsters.

Role-playing offers the closest substitute to naturally occurring human events and is a tool which parents and teachers of preschool children can use to great advantage. Perceptive parents who take their cue from the favored play-learning activities of their three-to-five-year-olds will intuitively recognize the superior impact of play-acting over discussion with preschool children, no matter how articulate those children may seem.

On the opposite end of the spectrum from parents in Bloom's study are parents who choose not to attend to the special talents of their children. A widespread anti-elitist sentiment in America leads many parents in the middle and lower classes to resist the identification of their child as intellectually gifted. In these cases, parents overlook early signs of self-awareness of difference in their children and avoid any overt discussion of superior abilities. They want their children to be "normal."

This parental attitude can have undesirable outcomes for the gifted child. The child's special abilities will not go away simply as a result of being ignored. For the child, these talents *are* normal, an inextricable component of self. The child is left to try and sort out for himself the environmental and social consequences and implications of his own above average abilities.

The differences will be experienced by the child, but he will have few opportunities to work them through or discuss them with the most important people in his world, his mother and father.

Students of human behavior have observed that an ignoring response is not a neutral response. It is a power negative response and one which behavior therapists use extensively in reducing unwanted behaviors in a child. Parents who choose to pay no attention to unique abilities in a child are sending that child a message every bit as strong as that of proud Grandpa in the restaurant. "These abilities are not pleasing to us and we are not interested in this aspect of your being."

A young child in such a setting perceives that being like everyone else is the most important priority. This can and does lead the young child to begin very early to hide those differences, those special abilities, from everyone. She may also perceive herself as odd or weird becaue of her special abilities and very confused about both possessing them and using them. And so her own discovery of the treasure of her individuality will be clouded and inhibited by her inability to explore her selfhood freely and to benefit from honest supportive interaction with understanding parents.

Some gifted children learn, even before they encounter the social buffeting of the schoolroom, to act ordinary and suppress their gifts. This may result in heightened peer acceptance and avoidance of challenge for the parents, but it constitutes phoney behavior for the child. What the child has learned is not a considered adaptation of her behavior to an evaluated situation but a consistent pattern of falsification of self. The comfortable obscurity of mediocrity is a high price to pay for the loss in personal growth that can ensue.

Equality of opportunity should provide for the full exploration of all an individual's abilities. It does not and should not predict equal performance.

A gifted child has a right to acceptance of these gifts on the part of parents and support in the discovery of the best way to use those gifts, both for self and others. The relationship between parent and child is the most important factor in the development of good feelings, toward self, and toward the rest of the world.

Below are some guidelines that parents should follow with young children as they discover themselves:

1. Examine your own value systems regarding child-rearing, personal fulfillment, and giftedness in American society. Ideally, personal introspection will be followed by parental discussion and mutual clarification of values.

2. Be honest. All children are sensitive to hypocrisy, no matter how well-meant, and gifted children are even more so.

3. Consider the developmental level of the child. Verbal interchange, even with a precociously articulate youngster, is not the most efficient path to genuine understanding for the preschool child.

4. Avoid lengthy explanation or discussions. It is easy for parents to overstate their case.

5. Be timely in responding to cues from the child. These may take the form of direct questions about differing ability or behaviors which indicate an awareness of differences.

6. Respect the personhood of the child. Avoid projecting your own career interests and desires onto your children.

4

Family Awareness

S IBLING RIVALRY is a nearly universal family condition, certainly
not unique to families of gifted youngsters. All families experience tensions between brothers and sisters as individual family
members find it necessary and desirable to adjust their own wants
and needs to the interests and demands of other family members.
When personalities are quite different, these adjustments are often
difficult, and age seniority is frequently invoked.

It sometimes happens that one child in a family constellation
is noticeably more intellectually gifted or artistically talented than
the others. When such a child is more able than older siblings, the
parents must exercise special tact and sensitivity in guiding the
family discovery process. Parents who report the least jealousy
describe homes in which the entire family has treated the giftedness of any of their children as something for the whole family to
enjoy. They take similar family pride in all of each other's achievements in no matter which area, truly family treasures.

One activity which the parents I work with have found especially rewarding is to sit down together in a family group and
actually write down the things about each other that they enjoy
the most and then share those things with each other—a mutual
admiration society, if you will.

For some reason, we all seem to find it much easier, or more
urgent, to let others know what they are doing that displeases us
than to tell them when they have made us glad. It may be a Puritan
or Calvinist heritage, but Americans seem more readily to describe

negative than positive feelings, to criticize more often than to praise.

Some families do sit down together to work through family problems. Children would probably respond more positively to such sessions if they were occasionally held in the absence of problems. Parents cannot take it for granted that children know how special Mom and Dad think each one is, any more than Dad can take it for granted that Mom knows he loves her. Both want to be reassured, specifically and often, and so do our children. Brothers and sisters squabble often but almost never tell each other what they like about each other. Parents need to model such behaviors, both with each other and with each child.

Encourage siblings to talk about their feelings directly with a more able brother or sister. It can bring them much closer together. Both parties will probably feel more comfortable if a parent is present as a buffer, since both negative and positive feelings will probably be shared on different occasions, and parents provide emotional security to youngsters trying out new ways to relate to each other. Emphasize mutual respect, compassion, and understanding. Model these behaviors as powerful ingredients of desirable socioemotional growth.

Parents should also recognize their own gifts. When interviewing parents of gifted youngsters, I ask them if they were gifted children themselves. They usually say they were not, although they often go on to describe experiences which most of us would recognize as evidence of exceptional ability. Our egalitarian social climate prevents them, especially the women, from acknowledging their own special gifts. As they encourage their children to discover themselves and to feel good about themselves, it is salutary for parents to be realistic in their own recognition of their talents and the unique contributions each makes to family synergy.

How do parents let their children know that they are valued for themselves, in all aspects of their being, rather than for their special area of giftedness? By valuing the special qualities in each child and focusing on the good in each. There are many human qualities which we treasure—a sunny disposition, generous spirit, helpfulness, patience, uncritical acceptance of others, energy, responsibility, dependability, integrity, and the power to make us laugh. Each family member can make a list of the special positive qualities of other family members, and parents can focus on these in family interactions as they reinforce individuality in each child.

A garden provides a homely analogy which may help children to understand and value differences. Different plants bloom at different seasons, some spread low and some shoot up high, but each contributes to the harmony of the whole. Tulips are not roses, forsythias are not geraniums, daisies are not orchids; and wouldn't our gardens be boring if they were! No mention has been made about the glories of lettuce, eggplant, and tomatoes which also make estimable contributions to the garden. A perfume, color, or flavor which is highly prized by one family member may be less desirable to another. Individual preferences in this neutral domain can also provide analogies for differences in interests and personalities at a more emotionally charged level.

One family found the concept of sibling synergy to be a productive and profitable framework for brother and sister cooperation. Synergy is a word which means that the whole is greater than the sum of its parts. The Laitin children, Ken, Steve, and Lindy, put together their experiences and gifts in a problem-solving approach to organized sports for youngsters in *The World's #1 Best Selling Soccer Book*. With Ken and Steve writing and Lindy illustrating, they dealt with such universal issues as:

1. What to do with the glory hog.
2. How to play against someone twice your size.
3. What to do when the other guys play dirty.

(I have lately been informed that "guys" is a non-sexist generic rather than a masculine term.)

This book is available commercially from:

Soccer for Americans
Box 836
Manhattan Beach, California 90266

Each child participated fully in the creation of the book, according to his or her gifts, and the final product was much more successful than any separate manuscript, individually written, might have been.

PART II
Nurturance

5

Special Strengths and Special Vulnerabilities

PARENTS of gifted children need to play a protective role as their youngsters begin to demonstrate outstanding abilities. Both the larger society and most schools have generally been uncomfortable with, even distrusted, the gifted child, because of his or her not-too-well-understood uniqueness. Parents are often unsure or uneasy, too, in an American society which has emphasized the average, glorifying the common man. Schools frequently maintain that gifted children need no help from others because they are sufficiently talented to guide themselves. This has certainly not been the experience of parents as they respond to the daily challenges of nurturing their gifted offspring. In fact, the needs of such children for emotional security, independence, achievement, recognition, and a sense of worth are often greatly frustrated more greatly even than those of handicapped youngsters. Because of a widespread distrust of those who are different, gifted children are often rejected by other children, by teachers, and sometimes even by parents.

The following interchange between the author and a concerned parent is more typical than one would like:

Having listened to the detailing of precocious behaviors of a four-year-old girl whose parents were seeking guidance in providing enrichment experiences for their very bright daughter, the author asked, "And have you any other children?" "Oh, yes," came the prompt reply. "She has a two-year-old sister, but, thank God, she seems to be normal!" expressed in a tone of palpable relief.

Such feelings get communicated to children in subtle and unsubtle ways. I did not ask if the four-year-old was in earshot of my telephoner, but if she overheard she received a confusing message about parental acceptance of her unique qualities.

The sense of obligation or inadequacy that many parents of gifted children express takes much of the fun out of parenting. With all its challenges and demands, there should be plentiful rewards, the foremost being the pleasure of living with such fascinating people as our gifted children can be. They are probably the most interesting individuals we will be privileged to know, like us and yet unlike us, new configurations of human traits formed from chance blendings of the strengths and weaknesses of both parents. The richness and diversity of their personalities are a daily inspiration. A healthy concern for the realization of potential should not be overemphasized to the point of constricting anxiety which inhibits the mutual enjoyment of parent and child.

SPECIAL STRENGTHS

In Chapter 1, on the multidimensionality of giftedness, many of the characteristics of gifted children were described. Their heightened abilities produce both special strengths and special vulnerabilities in these youngsters.

The sensory perceptions from their surroundings which they are able to take in, attend to, and interpret at any given point are more numerous and intense than for average children. They see more, hear more, and feel more than most others in the same settings. They can attend to several events simultaneously. They seldom "miss a trick." These perceptions include cues in the voice, posture, and behaviors of other people in their environment. Gifted children have been compared to sponges, soaking up sensations from all directions. This strength in *receptivity* leads to the vulnerability of *acute sensitivity*. These children pick up on everything and react to everything. Their normal egocentrism also leads them to refer everything around them to themselves. The slings and arrows of everyday interactions which glide harmlessly over the unaware head or off the shrugged shoulders of their companions can strike the gifted youngster to the quick. They assume guilt where no blame was conveyed. They feel rebuffed where no slight was intended.

Casual comments are internalized as personal criticisms. They are extraordinarily sensitive to the displeasure of adults around them and usually attribute it to something they themselves have done. Parents and playmates are sometimes surprised at what seem to be disproportionately extreme reactions to apparently minor events.

In conferences about their bright youngsters, parents will exclaim, "Oh, if only he weren't so sensitive," or, "I wish she weren't so easily hurt." Parents recognize the child's vulnerability and wish that they could lessen the possibility of pain. But that would mean a dulling also of the sensitivity to harmony and beauty and a lessening of the possibility of joy.

Understanding the positive as well as the negative con- comitants of such finely tuned perception, parents will be able to respond with more calm and patience to the emotional ups and downs which their young gifted offspring endure. Their children can be helped to see that not all disparaging comments are di- rected at them personally and that people sometimes speak and act thoughtlessly, without intent to wound.

People are more often careless or callous than cruel. And their occasional cruelty is often unintended.

In the breadth of their perception and sensitivity, gifted chil- dren learn about and care deeply about social injustices occurring both in America and world-wide. They feel confused and frustrated by their own perceptions of grievous wrongs that cry out to be righted and their personal inability to do anything about it. Leta Hollingsworth (1927) has said it well: "He whose grasp chronically exceeds his reach is always under a strain." It is a challenge for world-weary parents to respond to the gifted child's fervent desires to redress the unfairnesses of society. Without such desires and dreams in our youngsters, little social reform would be possible, and we do not want to stifle those dreams. Find some way in which the child or the family can respond even in a small way, writing letters, joining an action group, contributing from an allowance, to a cause that the child feels is just. And help her to be patient with less percipient others who do not share her urgency of concern. Such parental guidance helps to shape the social leaders of the future. We need to husband such resources.

A wise mentor of gifted went on to warn us, "a lesson which many highly intelligent persons never learn as long as they live is that human beings in general are incorrigibly very different from them in thought, action, and desire." In 1942 she wrote: "Many a reformer has died at the hands of a mob which he was trying to improve. The highly intelligent child must learn to suffer fools gladly—not sneeringly, not angrily, not despairingly, not weepingly—but gladly, if personal development is to proceed successfully in the world as it is" (Hollingsworth).

Failure to develop patient and amiable tolerance for the less able generality of people often leads to bitterness, disillusionment, and misanthropy, which are the ruin of potential leaders. Recall that one of the valued character traits, mentioned in Chapter 2 was uncritical acceptance of others. For some fortunate individuals, this seems to be an inborn facet of personality; for many intellectually gifted children it is a trait which must be learned. Parents do well to examine their own modeling behaviors in this regard.

But children can be cruel, and against intended cruelty none of us has adequate defenses. Parents cannot prevent all hurt to their children, but they can soften some of the impact and support a tempering of the egocentric developmental tendency to refer all causality to the self.

Another strength that is often noted is tremendous perseverance in areas of high interest. One of the earliest clues to giftedness is the intensity of length of involvement with an activity which parents observe in two- or three-year-olds. Little children can sometimes be engrossed for hours at a stretch and return to an activity over periods of several days, much longer than might be expected for a child of that age. As they grow older, gifted children demonstrate great tenacity and single-mindedness in completion of tasks that they have set themselves such as hobbies or projects.

This high level of task commitment contributes to worrisome *perfectionist tendencies* in many gifted children. These overly-high personal standards and resulting frustration when performances may fall short of expectations is the vulnerability associated with the strength of *high task commitment.*

A perfectionist tendency is among the problems most frequently mentioned by parents and teachers of the gifted. Many of us have seen quite praiseworthy products crumpled into the wastebasket because of minor flaws. School assignments laboriously worked over are consigned to oblivion at the bottom of a locker because they did not come up to the student's expectation of a desirable piece of work. The superior discriminatory powers of gifted students often lead them to judge their own work too harshly, applying the standards of the mature exponent of the particular field of endeavor. They inflict on themselves apparently needless pain and frustration in their paralyzing dissatisfaction with any performance short of their internalized image of excellence.

Parents can intensify negative feelings about self with such well-meant remarks as, "This is good, but we know you can do it better," or "Were there others who scored higher?" and similar often-reported comments in response to children's performances. If adult expectations are too high or too difficult to sustain, the child will see himself as a failure in their eyes and consequently, in his own.

Excessive ambition in parents has been noted by Freeman (1980) to be associated with noticeably high levels of hostility in their children.

But whence this driving need to excel? Here parents must examine closely the reinforcement system within the home. Many parents and doting grandparents unwittingly feed the gifted youngster's perfectionist tendencies.

Child development specialists and common sense both tell us that we each do what pays off for us. The behaviors that result in our obtaining responses that make us feel loved and competent are the behaviors that we will repeat and refine in order to receive more reinforcement or pay-offs.

When we ask what the most rewarding thing is for babies, toddlers, school-age children, we realize that it is attention from beloved parents. Aware that their attention, and especially pleased attention, is such a powerful shaper of the child's behavior, it behooves all parents to take careful stock of their own attention-giving patterns with each child.

One of the strongest drives which a young child has is the drive to please parents, which is closely related to another drive, to be like the parent. How does the child figure out what pleases the parent? By noting closely and filing under top priority those events which bring a smile, an approving nod, a special gleam in the eye, a proud note in the voice of that most significant person, Mom or Dad. This process begins very early and is extremely powerful.

When a child is blessed with a unique potential and demonstrates precocious abilities, it is understandable that a parent or grandparent might give a great deal of attention and praise in response to those behaviors in which the child excels greatly in comparison to age-mates. These are the events which are fondly described to relatives and friends. These are the behaviors that the child is asked to repeat for visitors. And without deliberate intention on the part of parents, the child perceives that what pleases the parent most is that behavior which excels. The legitimate pride of the parents, when demonstrated without the balance of pleasurable attention to other desirable behaviors, feeds the roots of the perfectionist tendencies which later can cause problems for many gifted children. The child learns that to excel, to be the best, is what gets most positive parental attention. Participation in an activity for simple enjoyment of the activity is not reinforced. Excelling is what counts.

Ruth Duskin Feldman (1982) relates: "When I was encouraged to do *my* best, it became, in my mind, to be *the* best."

Return to the earlier suggestion of thoughtful examination of personal, parental values. Describe the range of desirable human qualities that contribute to successful living. How many there are in addition to intellectual ability, physical or artistic talents! We have mentioned patience, dependability, helpfulness, honesty, generosity, and many others.

Through the course of several days examine those times in which you give attention to your child. Keep a little journal record or diary. Are you, in your reinforcing behaviors, communicating the priorities which you genuinely hold? Or have you given disproportionate attention to the gift and to the area of excelling, neglecting to reward the other satisfying aspects of your child's personal development? Our behaviors tell our children what is important to us about them. The behaviors they then invest the most energy in, either to please us or punish us, are the most telling evidence of how they have interpreted our priorities.

If they perceive that excellence in individual performance is to be what the parent values most, because it gets the most attention, then they will strive hardest toward being the best in everything they do and feel not only frustrated but guilty whenever they fall short. Not excelling is letting parents down and letting parents down makes children feel guilty. One of the most negative examples is the outrageous behavior of some ego-involved parents when their youngsters are involved in little-league types of sports activities. We decry such excesses but we may be unconsciously doing similar but less extreme things in giving too much attention to excelling in our gifted children.

This is not to suggest that their gifts and triumphs should be ignored, but that we maintain a healthy balance in what we attend to in all areas of development, lest our children misinterpret parental priorities and internalize a mistaken need to be the best, to be perfect, in order to please parents, and consequently, to feel good about themselves.

Children need early experiences of reward for trying, even when they don't succeed, reward for risk-taking even when the outcome is off the mark, reward for participating as well as for winning. Otherwise they will choose early to engage themselves only in their areas of excellence and avoid any activities in which they may not be the best.

The ability to perceive and make fine discriminations of quality is an innate strength, but the need for perfection is a *learned* vulnerability with very mixed results for the child.

The wide-ranging curiosity of gifted children is another strength which is noticed early by parents. This curiosity drive has been described by Robert White (1959) as an inborn trait of human infants, a need to experience the environment, to manipulate the environment, and to find meaning in the environment. The great student of child development, Jean Piaget, who began his scientific career as a biologist, likened the working of the human mind to the functioning of the human organic systems. The human nervous system needs stimulation as desperately as the lungs need air to supply the blood with oxygen and the alimentary system needs foodstuffs to supply the body with amino acids and glycogen. It is as natural for the brain to learn as for other organs to breathe, eat, and drink. The most uncomfortable state of being for the human organism is not hunger, thirst, fatigue, sexual deprivation, or even physical pain. We can postpone eating, sleeping, rest, and comfort when we are involved in an activity that is intensely interesting. The condition most intolerable to human beings is boredom! Children and adults will go to great lengths to escape boredom, reading the labels on bathroom cleanser containers or seeking a numerical sequence of license plate numbers to add interest to routine drives. Just as children have a right to sufficient food to nurture bodily development, they have a right to sufficient stimulation to nurture mental development. Children have a right not to be bored!

This appetite for intellectual stimulation and novelty is commonly called curiosity, and our gifted youngsters with their breadth of cognitive potential have voracious appetites for new experiences to feed their developing minds.

The vulnerabilities associated with this strength of *diversity of interests* include *starting too many things at once,* often out of a fear of missing any activitiy that might be stimulating, and *assaying projects that are too global* for the time, energy, and present expertise of the child.

Both of these situations lead to frustrations in the child which must be responded to by both parents and teachers. Gifted youngsters need to learn to strike a balance between enthusiasm and pragmatism. This balance, which seems to come only through experience, is called prudence. Prudence is not included in the cornucopia of gifts with which children may be endowed. It is essentially a learned virtue and not one that appears particularly attractive to exploring, creative youngsters. There is also the possibility that it may have been overlearned by many life-scarred parents and adult mentors. The goal is to find a felicitous middle path that encourages risk-taking exploration but reduces the probability of paralyzing frustration of frequent failure.

Two skills which experience engenders in parents and which are vital factors in guarding the potential for healthy productivity in their gifted children are setting priorities and clarifying focus. In the first instance, it is helpful to join with a child in examining a realistic time schedule which includes family responsibilities as well as individual interests, not forgetting sleep. A gifted child may enjoy doing a detailed time study for a week in order to get a clear picture of how his minutes and hours are spent. Don't be surprised if he also does time studies on parental activities. It might be a good idea if, before suggesting this to a child, the parents conduct their own individual time studies in order to examine their own priorities and productivity. This would also be an excellent opportunity for a parent to provide a role model that encourages the child to "Do as I do, in support of as I say."

Looking at a weekly journal in this way may alert parents to such common pitfalls as overscheduling the gifted child's time in structured lessons and activities. This leaves little opportunity for spontaneous experiences, daydreaming space, self-directed activities, and activities which contribute to self-knowledge and future independence.

There may be concomitant alerting in examination of a parental journal to a possible inconsistency in priorities and time use, especially time with each child. It should be noted here that, in interviews with gifted school-age youngsters, a frequent response to the question "If you could change one thing at home, what would it be?" was to have more time with a parent. In our efforts to do more *for* our children, are we forgetting the need to do things *with* our children? Nor should parents neglect personal introspection time, time for the examined life.

The desired outcome is a considered allocation of time and energy to valued interests that allows a high likelihood of eventual satisfactory task completion in each area.

A companion skill is that of clarifying focus. A widely reported problem with gifted children is that they envision a desirable project too globally. They want to encompass all there is to know about a given topic because it is all related, and it is all interesting. This is attractive in its intent but ultimately frustrating in its implementation. Pragmatic reality enforces itself and there is only so much time in which to complete the project. The prudence of experience can be brought to the guidance function of helping the young knowledge-seeker to narrow her focus and delimit a do-able segment from the possible scope of an inviting inquiry. This skill also helps to curb the pervasive tendency of the student to keep on looking and reading (which are fun) as she postpones writing (which is work).

Most young learners initiating a project at home or at school need a very flexible exploratory phase during which they identify major ideas, big questions, and inquiry strategies or experimental methods. Here the adult helps best by providing resources. It is in the second phase, selection of emphasis and winnowing of specifics, that the adult can provide the leading questions and guiding suggestions that help the child give the project a framework that provides for satisfactory closure within a reasonable time. It should not be a closing off of possible ramifications and avenues of inquiry, but rather a pacing of involvement that lessens frustration. There will be a tomorrow for further investigation.

Prudent narrowing of the scope of a project also helps to prevent abandonment of the good work given to an inquiry because the disparate components may not come together to the individual satisfaction of the perfectionist youngster. The vulnerabilities overlap, as do the ameliorative responses.

An obvious special strength of gifted and talented children is that *they succeed in nearly everything they attempt* and that they excel in some or many areas. This would seem to predict a strong positive self-concept, but in life we encounter disturbing paradoxes. The vulnerability that accompanies the experience of excelling is an *inability to accept non-excelling.* Many gifted children, aware of superior abilities, see anything other than first as a failure and have negative feelings about themselves whenever they are not at the top. Their experience-derived expectations for self are so high that they frequently disappoint themselves and develop poor self-concepts.

Parents can guard against this vulnerability of inability to adjust wholesomely to a place in the pack by making sure that their children are involved early and with reasonable frequency in activities in which they do not excel. Giftedness is not next to godliness (nor is cleanliness). But if we encourage or allow our highly talented offspring to participate only in activities in which they do excel, and if we place priority on being best rather than on the pleasure of the activity or the company, then we can foster such a deleterious misconception. Large numbers, in fact the majority, of students interviewed at one of our most selective colleges expressed feelings of inferiority. Their performance fell short—or they feared it would fall short—of their parents' expectations (Strang 1960).

One can find, even in the devotees of such an apparently noncompetitive avocation as bird-watching, differences between the enjoyers of birds and listers of birds. When the length of the list rather than the pleasure of observing natural phenomena becomes the primary concern, then we are seeing an adult example of the need to be best overriding the intrinsic worth of the activity and the fellow participants.

Many families of gifted youngsters encourage their children to take part in physical activities, some of which they enjoy as a family, in drama, dance, carpentry, gardening, or perhaps volunteering in social agencies. Children with outstanding abilities need also to experience a modicum of mediocrity on occasion in order to solidify their ties with the struggling majority. They will gain both in patience with others and in understanding of self.

It is human to learn that it is all right, even expected, that one fails occasionally. Failure should be an occasion for reassessment and adaptation, not for despair and self-denigration. To the seeker after new information or new friends, the message "That didn't work" can be as useful as the message "That works." We should share with our children in ways that help them to profit from both messages, to be open to experiences that may not lead to the laurels.

Participation in team-based physical activities is often a problem for gifted youngsters who are not blessed with superior physical prowess. When these non-athletic children are asked why they play so little, their usual response is that they are not picked for a team because they have poor coordination, they don't play well enough. When age peers of these youngsters are asked why these same individuals are not tapped for the team, they report that it is because they are such poor sports, they can't stand to lose. They spoil the fun.

Intellectually gifted youngsters are apparently able to fool themselves or rationalize their rejection by others and avoid confronting the real reasons for not being accepted in team play. The strength of their experiences in excelling does not provide them with socially acceptable responses to losing. This *poor loser* vulnerability is best counteracted by encouraging involvement early in the broadest possible range of activities which will foster the child's awareness of a wide range of talents in self and others.

The experience of losing and the feelings associated with being bested will also furnish the best antidote to being a *poor winner* and cockily belittling the efforts of the less successful.

A related vulnerability, low social skills, will be discussed at greater length in the following chapter.

It would be worthwhile and interesting to study sport participation at the burgeoning number of summer camps for gifted kids where both mental and physical exercise opportunities are offered.

I wonder sometimes about the wisdom in the current effort to take the recognition systems traditionally associated with athletics and transfer them to academic achievement. In an attempt to give equal public recognition to both, may we not be taking some of the most pernicious competitive aspects of organized athletics and incorporating them in intellectual pursuits? Is competition, an olympiad of the mind, what we truly seek to foster? A television special describing the Olympics of the Mind program (now called Odyssey of the Mind) highlighted this issue for me in a debate among participants on one of the young teams. One girl who insisted that they were in it for the learning experience and that the important thing was to enjoy it was scornfully rejected by a male teammate who insisted that he was in it to win—that winning was the only important thing and that without such an attitude, participation would be meaningless. Most of the team members were then swept up in that desire to win. I have serious misgivings about the clearly well-meant support, even in the name of equity of recognition, for organized activities for gifted children which foster winning for its own sake. Those with whom I have discussed this concern over the years usually indicate that competition is a condition of the real world and a necessary component of "making it" in American society. Is that a reason for intensifying competitiveness? Crime is also a condition of the real world but not one we like to regard as a necessary component of American society. Other cultures place much greater emphasis on cooperation, an alternative that, if fostered in the young, might benefit American society. It would have to start at home, with parents ceasing to make comparisons between brothers and sisters, cousins and neighbors, which lead the child to compete in order to please.

Many of the teachers with whom I have worked indicate that they believe the competitive drive is innate, like the curiosity drive. They believe this because they see it operating already in the little ones as they enter school. But I believe that it is simply learned early in the bosom of the family or in the Diaper Derbies annually televised from shopping malls where the race course is measured off and the baby who crawls the fastest from Mommy to Daddy gets the cheers and an edible gold medal, a cookie on a ribbon.

Excessive competitiveness can be easily and perhaps unintentionally fostered in gifted children by immoderate parental attention to winning for its own sake. Efforts should be made to redirect competitiveness toward comparisons with one's own past performances, striving for self-improvement, and achieving personal competence, rather than striving to outperform and outshine others. The intrinsic reinforcement of achieving a personal best can be made much more attractive to a sensitive, gifted youngster than the extrinsic reinforcement of adulation for winning a contest.

Another unique strength of gifted children is the *ability to perceive relationships*. They see unthought-of connections between concepts, between events. These relationship often form the basis of creativity and inventiveness. The vulnerability enters in when these *unique perceptions lead the child down untried paths*. Conventional wisdom and customs of tradition suggest that the new path may be foolish, useless, or dangerous, and pressures may be brought to bear on the youngster to avoid wasting time in frivolous pursuits.

Suggestions for new and more efficient ways to do things are often rejected in favor of the tried and true. Parents who wish to guard against the loss of creativity and willingness to innovate will be flexible in their child-rearing practices and open to the possibility of the child's way being a better way. It does happen.

No discussion of the strengths of gifted children can omit the one which probably supports these youngsters through all the vicissitudes and vulnerabilities we have been describing. That is their wonderful *sense of humor*. They perceive so much; their imaginations are so active; they are so playful; and so they find incongruities and fun in many places. Parents often report this trait as one of the delights of living with gifted children. Finding humor in awkward or painful situations is a primary ego defense mechanism for gifted youngsters, one which parents can support but not be fooled by. Laughter is used sometimes to hide big hurts, and parents need to be sensitive and understanding even while they are smiling with the child who is laughing to keep from crying.

This marvelous ability to see humor in diverse situations is often the key to social acceptance by peers. We are familiar with the highly gifted learner as class clown, better to be a joker than an egghead. Sensitive teachers know that, in their quest for normal popularity, superior children often disguise their intellectual abilities as soon as they leave the primary grades. But not the sparkle of their wit! Bright underperformers can find their protective camouflage wasted on wise teachers who recognize the puns, pranks, and caricatures as clues to unused potential. It takes a sensitive as well as knowledgeable teacher to coax out the interest and involvement of these youngsters who have learned by experience that it's not cool to be smart in most classrooms. The gifted child's motives for underachieving must be explored and understood.

A sense of humor is also a vital strength for the parents and teachers of exceptionally able youngsters. Being the only person in a given setting who sees the joke, so to speak, can make for vulnerability. This does happen with gifted children whose classmates or teachers are not tuned in to the multiple perceptions and relationships with which bright children love to play. A number of gifted children who were asked about their best friends reported the basis of friendship as shared humor: "We think the same things are funny, even when no one else does." A panel of junior high school gifted youngsters at a regional conference indicated that the trait they most valued in teachers was a sense of humor. Laughing together should strengthen families as well as friendships.

6

Responding to Problem Behaviors

I N GUARDING the province of childhood, parents need to prevent children's positive qualities from being deflected into inappropriate behaviors. Gifted children can be deficient in social skills and functional social behaviors. They need help in developing the ordinary amenities of interaction among people—patience, courtesy, respect for elders. Interests of their age peers, sports, and popular music are also legitimate, and it is socially advantageous for them to show a polite interest in the goals and activities of others.

Their intellectual acuity makes gifted children capable of analyzing their own behavior, but their normal developmental egocentrism causes them to need more mature assistance in understanding how some of their behaviors affect others. Gifted children exhibit a cluster of fairly common behavior patterns which frequently cause rejection by peers, teachers, and sometimes other family members. The problem areas most often reported in surveys of teachers and counselors of the gifted and talented include interrupting, correcting, know-it-all, and mockery.

The parent who understands the unique abilities of the child and the superior strengths that often prompt interactions unacceptable to others who may be slower on the uptake will be better equipped to guide the child in self-understanding in the service of changing the undesirable behavior. If the child sees that the parent can cut through to the underlying goodness of the intent (most people strive for the good as they see it), then the child is more open to the suggestions of that parent. Parental suggestions should include examples of desirable alternate behaviors which are reasonable to the child and, importantly, modeled by the parents. As we read further in this chapter, some of us may recognize bits of ourselves, both as children and adults.

Interruption when others are talking is one of the most often cited of unpleasant behaviors of the gifted. Why are bright children so prone to interrupting others when they speak? Sometimes they are already familiar with what is being said and are able to complete the speaker's thought for themselves before the speaker's utterance is completed. They then burst forth with a response prematurely. Sometimes, even when the material is new, they can leap ahead to the implications before the speaker has completed a proposition, and they are eager to demonstrate their understanding, again prematurely. The perceived prematurity of the interrupting response is the result of the more average rates of comprehension of the speaker and other listeners, as well as a breach of the turn-taking behavior that conversational mores prescribe. There is also a conjecture emerging both from researcher's experiences (Gowan 1972; Meeker 1978) and current advances in understanding the biochemistry and electrical charges in the brain, that some thought transference or telepathy takes place between strong transmitters and receivers who are on the same channels. The child may be getting the speaker's message before it is spoken.

In each of these conditions, the child usually assumes that all other hearers in the environment are receiving and processing at a similar rate and would also interact at a similar tempo if they wished to.

The child's attention to the speaker, his understanding of the speaker's message content, and his desire to interact are all positive traits that should be recognized and praised. Then parents must explain what the child has failed to realize. Most others, often including the speaker, do not pick up on things, understand, or remember with the same speed and facility as the gifted interrupter. It is helpful to emphasize that each of the others has the need and the right (tap into the child's strong sense of fairness) to come to his or her own mental closure and understanding of the speaker's message, that this can take more time for others, and the child should not begrudge this time. Recall to the child his own joy and satisfaction in coming to solutions or realizations on his own, how he hates to be supplied with an answer before he has figured it out for himself. For the very young child, it might be necessary to role play a sample situation or take advantage of occasions of interrupting behavior when he is the victim in order for him to be able to examine experientially the feelings of the interrupted. An older youngster can understand the truncation of the learning experience which occurs when answers are too readily supplied. The problem behavior usually arises because the bright child is unaware that others are thinking more slowly, or in his youthful enthusiasm, he forgets. His behavior is then experienced by others as rude and impatient.

The loving parent will remind the child about prior discussions of differential abilities and indicate how these differences seem to be contributing to social misunderstandings. Then encourage the child to be patient, to cultivate this virtue which is often lacking in the gifted. Practice patience yourself in interaction with your child and be quick to praise her when she practices it herself, when she refrains from interrupting and graciously gives brothers, sisters, classmates, or parents ample opportunity to complete their spoken thoughts. Her patience will be more often prized by others than her ebullience and may also help her to develop more patience with herself.

Another aspect of interrupting that might be discussed with older children is the psychological interpretation people attach to interrupting. It is seen by most adults as a power move, an assertion of control by the interrupter over the interrupted. The person who is interrupted feels threatened by the one who has interrupted, or, at the very least, resentul at the implied intent to challenge. Aware of this possible effect on others, youngsters can consider whether they wish to be perceived by others as challenging or threatening. They usually decide otherwise.

Often the cognitive abilities of gifted children far outpace their social understanding, and they benefit a great deal from the counsels of a wise and caring adult whom they trust.

A related behavior, which is not really interrupting but results in similar resentment from peers and sometimes in irritation from teachers, is always being the first to shoot up a hand whenever teacher asks a question. A sensitive child of seven or eight will notice negative reactions to his consistent and immediate volunteering and share his puzzlement with parents. "Why does the teacher tell me to put my hand down?" "Why do the other kids give me dirty looks?" "Doesn't the teacher want to see who knows the answer?" etc.

And so it is time to talk to him about weighing alternatives and making choices. The parent can respond with some related questions. Weighing alternatives:

> "Do you think that by now the teacher probably knows you will know the answer?"
> "Have you thought that sometimes the teacher's question is to stimulate everyone's thinking and an immediate answer would close off your classmates' thinking time?"
> "Are you giving others an opportunity to volunteer first some of the time?"

And the hard choice:

> "Is it more important for you to be liked by others, to have your friends in your class, or to show the teacher that you know the answer?"

If building friendships and stopping those dirty looks is the first priority, and it usually is for eight-year-olds, then offer this suggestion: Practice patience. When you know the answer right away, wait and glance around you. If you have counted to ten and no classmate has raised a hand then maybe this is one of those times when it's better not to single yourself out. And the teacher needs to work some more so that others can know the answer.

Teachers can also help children who are experiencing this difficulty. Some teachers arrange to have the exceptionally able child or children simply write down those quick answers and leave the paper with her at the end of the day (or class). Thus, the student is not discouraged from responding, nor is he or she conspicuous in the group. Some such strategies can be extremely important in maintaining both academic motivation and social acceptance, especially for adolescent girls. As one junior high daughter told her parents: "It's bad enough to be taller than the boys, but if you're smarter, that's death!"

There is evidence that some equally gifted interlocutors are not hampered by apparent interruptions. Two old friends lunching with a group of colleagues, all chatting after eating, were reprimanded by another companion as the two were engaged in an earnest conversation. "Why you're not even listening to each other—you're both talking at once!" But they were listening, understanding, and responding as they demonstrated in a playback of the conversation. In fact, they hadn't even realized that they were not pausing, taking turns, but were quite effectively communicating by talking together, a practice they had unconsciously fallen into which would not work so well in conversation with others.

Sometimes in families with several gifted children such congruent co-talking behavior develops and may be carried over unaware into other play or school settings where it does not work and is not socially acceptable.

A third and related form of interrupting often takes place when someone else in the group is telling a joke and the bright youngster blurts out the punch line—not because he has heard the joke before but because he sees what is coming and finds it funny. And so, out it tumbles and he has "stepped on my lines" and spoiled the joke for the teller. This is a hard behavior to modify because it is so spontaneous, but your gifted youngster will keep more friends if he can be helped to a heightened awareness of what he is doing and to more self-control in holding back the punch line and the laughter until the raconteur has finished the story in his own way.

A second commonly reported social irritant in the gifted youngster is the habitual correcting of others. How can such an unpleasant trait be rooted in any positive aspect of the developing personality? To help in understanding the emergence of correcting behavior, it is necessary to recall Piagetian egocentrism. This is the normal self-referent perspective which focuses all experience for young children. They believe, naively, that their thoughts, awareness, and feelings are shared by all persons in their immediate environment. (Even as adults we never totally outgrow this and it is often difficult to take another's point of view.)

One of the kinds of experiences that gifted children most frequently have is of "being right." They are praised, rewarded, for being right. They really like being right. Most of us do. For many gifted children the reverse is proportionately uncomfortable. They hate to be wrong! And they feel that every other person also would hate to be wrong. They genuinely wish to help others to avoid that painful state just as they wish to avoid it themselves. And so, if someone makes a mistake, they leap vigorously and promptly and publicly to her assistance, because of course she would not want to be wrong (ignominious state!).

The parent who understands the basic altruism combined with the childish egocentricity which produces this undesirable behavior can best help the offender by getting to the heart of the problem, the mistaken idea that the other person is as concerned about being wrong as the would-be correcter is. The state of being publicly corrected is much more painful than that of having made an error of pronunciation or information.

The virtue then that is being misdirected is that of kindness and the desire to forestall pain. Help your gifted child to understand that the greater kindness is to ignore the mistake and forestall the embarrassment of another. By correcting another, the gifted child is causing discomfort rather than preventing it, and provoking a great deal of resentment at the same time. Reinforce those occasions when your child shows kindness and forbearance. These are virtues that need to be cultivated and strengthened in gifted children, through positive parental attention.

Even a virtue can be carried too far. In a recent column letter, a very tender-hearted writer asked if in conversation another person mispronounces or misuses a word and the second speaker, in replying, has occasion to use the word correctly, is it more appropriate to repeat the first speaker's error in order to avoid embarrassing her, or to use the correct form. I believe that to be patronizing rather than kind, and really silly.

Another troubling epithet too often applied to gifted youngsters is "know-it-all," which refers to their aggravating tendency to appear to be one-upping their companions. As a concerned friend or parent observes children talking together and discusses with a confused youngster why her conversational gems are being so often rejected, a causal pattern emerges.

All children have a deep need to belong, to be accepted, to sense community. In their intense need to be in-the-swim, gifted children often respond to another child's excited anecdote with a description of a similar experience of their own. What frequently happens? The bright child usually has a better memory, a more vivid imagination, a richer vocabulary, a livelier sense of humor. Her story is often more interesting in color, detail, and expression. The first storyteller seems to be put in the shade by the apparent desire of the second to go her one better, to have done or seen everything the other had described, and perhaps, done it better.

Then rejection rather than belonging is the outcome, but the gifted child who is so precocious in verbal skills is often not at all advanced in social skills and does not understand the negative response to her overtures which were intended to convey similarity not superiority. She will make closer friends and evoke warmer relationships if she leaves center stage to the first narrator and gives her friend the luxury of unshared limelight. Her own story of a related experience can be shared at some future time when it will not be perceived by peers as directly competitive with the first narrator and the similarities of interest and response will not be overshadowed by resentment about being "one-upped."

The problem of verbal mockery usually has more complex roots, both in the extreme personal sensitivity of the gifted and talented and in their verbal skills. When your child seems to be constantly jibing and taunting playmates, brothers and sisters, even parents or teachers, look closely into his daily environment for possible pain sources. What is your own instinctual response when you are hurt—to hurt back; and if you can't wound the pain giver, you often flail out at the nearest target.

Gifted children are often stung by the attitudes and comments of playmates or unthinking adults. They over-internalize and over-apply the lightly made comments that roll harmlessly over the heads or off the shoulders of less-aware youngsters. Because gifted children perceive more, they are more susceptible, both to pleasure and pain.

When they are hurt they want to hurt back, and they have at their command two very powerful weapons—a rich store of language and well-honed insights into the vulnerabilities of friends and family. Their retaliatory verbal strikes then are often more damaging than the stimuli that so provoked the mocking response.

Talk to your youngster about the daily hurts which are often unintended. Sometimes, however, the negative attitudes and slights of others *are* intended, and that also should be talked out with your child. Offer a sympathetic ear to the outpouring of anger and resentment that may ensue and acknowledge the validity of the feeling of pain and social distress.

Help him to understand the destructive ways in which he is using his superior intuition and verbal skills. The old saying needs revision: "Sticks and stones may break my bones, but names will *always* hurt me."

The gifted child has learned that physical retaliation is frowned upon, that his verbal skills usually far exceed his physical prowess, and so he chooses to fight with words. Just as he has learned that in physical fights you are urged to "pick on someone your own size," he should be admonished to follow a parallel course in verbal altercations. Sarcasm is the brutality of the intellect and no one wants to be a bully.

Sometimes gifted youngsters demonstrate intellectual comprehension of abstract terms like justice, kindness, and charity, but they do not seem to make concrete applications in their daily lives. Parents need to help them to see the relationship of these beautiful ideas to the simple events of day-to-day living with other human beings.

Parents and teachers of gifted children become quite concerned about the amount and intensity of mockery, jeering, and biting sarcasm that sometimes develops among siblings or classmates. It is a distorted form of display of power, analogous to muscle-flexing and arm wrestling for those whose talents are more physical. This misuse of highly developed verbal skills, even in service of ego-preservation, should be discussed and discouraged as soon as it occurs. Writing it all down in a journal is one way of getting it out without causing excessive pain to others.

Hess and Shipman (1965) have studied child-rearing practices extensively. They tell us that parenting styles of directing children fall into two categories, imperative and instructive.

The imperative style is typified by unqualified commands, such as, "clean your room" and "sit down and be quiet."

The instructive style conveys more information and a command that carries with it a rationale for the desired behavior: "Put your toys on the shelf, your magazines in the basket, your dirty clothes in the hamper, and I'll run the vacuum while you make your bed," or "you will not have a single shirt or pair of socks to wear to school on Monday unless you gather up your clothes for the laundry," or "I'm trying to analyze this estimate for home energy conservation improvements, so please find something quiet to do until I'm finished and we can work on the birdfeeder."

The imperative style has been found to produce passive compliant approaches by the child and to foster dependence and conformity. It may bring about the desired behavior in the short term but will not contribute to the child's maturity. This style also may generate passive resistance. The child accedes to the command but then proceeds as s-l-o-w-l-y as possible to putter about at the task. The child wishes to avoid the outright confrontation involved in refusing the command and so sets up a psychological battle of attrition, "I am doing it" or "I'm still working on it, don't you see?" Mahatma Gandhi had no monopoly in the power of passive resistance.

Parents experiencing such dragging-it-on-forever performance in their youngsters may well examine their directive style as one possible source of the problem.

We may also consider our own reluctance to carry out some necessary but less-than-exciting tasks. As Joan Rivers says, "Why do wives have to spend so much time dusting, vacuuming, mopping, making beds, washing dishes, when you just have to do it all again six months later?"

The contrasting instructive style facilitates initiative and assertive approaches. It may also engender debate and open confrontation. Once the parent offers reasons for an activity, the child may counter with conflicting reasons or a rationale for doing a task in another way or at another time. Should this occur, the parents may ask themselves, "Why not let the child try it her way? It could be just as acceptable—or maybe even better." "What are the time constraints on this chore; could it just as well be done at another time? What is the child's higher priority?" The parent may decide against the child and indicate that some family priority carries more weight, but the child will have been heard.

And sometimes the parent may find the child's reasons informative and compelling. Bright kids sometimes see better ways of doing things, and if their approach won't work, it's important that they try things and find out for themselves, except in cases of danger to life, limb, or expensive equipment.

The instructive approach has been found to be associated with independence and creativity in youngsters. These virtues are not always the most comfortable for parents to live with, but they are the most interesting and challenging and promise most for the child's future.

There is a danger that parental concern for enhancing the child's special abilities may lead to an overscheduling of the child's time in lessons and performances and exclusion from the normal home and family responsibilities of other children, even within the same family. A parent should not consciously or unconsciously neglect other social and emotional aspects of development. The child needs regular duties and responsibilities within the normal routines of the home. It is important to find a happy medium between special lessons and homely chores shared by all family members.

In the search for the roots in virtue of many of the faults we see in our children, parenting gifted youngsters is not different from nurturing any children. But because their capabilities are superior, their dysfunctions can be powerfully irritating. Fortunately, they can understand these analyses of negative social behaviors when shared by a loving parent in a one-to-one situation and can usually modify behaviors that are putting people off and not bringing about their own desired outcomes.

Whenever a pattern of problem behavior emerges, consider what valid and laudable personal need or concern might be at the heart of the matter. Observe the day-to-day experiences, parents, school, playmates—even make some anecdotal records of events—to see if there is a discernible pattern of happenings in the environment that is hurting, frustrating, or angering the child. Keep central to your efforts to understand and respond to the behavior the realization that there is a striving for good underlying the apparent evil. Reach for the good and help the child to be a happier, more socially gifted person. Help him to develop the kinds of actions that attract and hold people rather than repel or defeat them. Nobody wants to be rejected. Parents can take positive action through a shared understanding of the desirable antecedents of undesirable behaviors and through the purposeful reinforcement of patience, kindness, modesty, and ego security. Building ego security is a primary function of the family and one which can only be adequately carried out in the warmth of the nurturing and supportive home.

There are dangers in focusing on problem behaviors of gifted children. Parents read about behavior disturbances of gifted children which are often sensationalized in the media—creating stereotypes—and then expect their own bright children to have them. "If my child doesn't exhibit these problems, does that mean that she is not gifted?" We should not overlook the large numbers of well-adjusted gifted children in our concern for the ones who are experiencing difficulties.

7

Building the Self-Concept

THE INFLUENCE of parents on the gifted child's concept of self cannot be overremphasized. It is a primary factor exerted during the child's most impressionable years. It is continuous, day after day, year following year. It pervades all aspects of the child's life and is intensified by its emotional tone. Parents are the significant others in the development of the child, and their every word and action carries enormous weight for the child. Anything a loved person says or does is particularly influential, and the parents are the center of the world for the baby and young child. The effect of early relationships persists throughout life.

The most significant aspect of the child's development which the parent is in the unique position of helping to shape is the child's sense of himself as a person.

Physical growth is nurtured by food which farmers and grocers provide and the exercise of muscles which are the normal activities of children. Intellectual stimulation can come from curious exploration of the environment, from books and other media and, of course, from teachers. Special talents can be enhanced by mentors, coaches, trainers, master teachers. There are many support systems outside the family which contribute resources that foster development. But none can replace the family in the nourishment of the child's psyche, the image of self as a competent and loved person, secure and happy in her own skin.

We form our ideas of who we are in interaction with the persons and experiences in our daily living. We receive both verbal and nonverbal messages about the worth of our activities, the attractiveness of our physical appearance, the pleasure of our company. In tiny day-to-day increments, parents send children messages about themselves. "You are strong," "You make me happy," "You can do that," "You are a big help," "You are so funny," "Tell me about what you're making," or "I know you can do that better," "It's so frustrating when you do that," "Here, let me do it for you," "I can do it faster myself," "Why do you have to act peculiar?" "Not now, dear, I'm reading."

Of course, the parent is going to give some negative communication to the child. That is how a child finds out about desirable and undesirable or safe and unsafe behavior. The important thing is the balance. Positive, encouraging, loving messages should far outweigh the critical ones.

The most important gift that you, and only you, can sponsor in your child is a secure sense of self as an effective contributor in a welcoming world.

Erik Erikson (1963) has made great contributions to our understanding of the psychosocial development of the individual. He tells us that the early foundations of a healthy personality are laid in the *trusting* relationship that develops in the first 24 months of life between the baby and the mother, or primary caregiver.

The consistency of response and the warmth of the interaction tell the infant that life is, on balance, good and the environment a safe and rewarding place. "I am wanted. My needs will be met. I have a special place here."

As the infant grows into early childhood, her cognitive development enables her to begin to differentiate between self and other, self and the world. She has been learning that she as an individual is a source of force, that she can manipulate her environment and make things happen. That is an exhilarating discovery, and she tries out her effectiveness with vigor: "Me do it, me!" She tests the power of her own will and her influence over people as well as objects: "No, won't do it," "Want to have that, now." She rejoices in realization of a newfound *autonomy* and mastery. And parents have been taught by well-meaning experts to call this challenging period the terrible twos. What would be terrible would be the absence of appearance of sense of self as an autonomous individual, of the ability to choose among options and reject some, of the promise of a healthy and independent ego in a self-directing, mature individual. Rather than bemoan the so-called stubbornness or negativism of the aware and articulate two-year-old, parents should take satisfaction in the child's growing competence and communicate their pride and enthusiasm as they lovingly set necessary limits to the scope or direction of the ambitious but unwary two-year-old. The baby is rapidly disappearing so that the toddler can take over. And the child says, "I'm me" and "I will" or "I won't!" The tremendous twos!

The next few years bring a widening of the child's horizons as activities and relationships extend beyond the family circle to the neighborhood, and often, nursery school or day care. The child's autonomy comes squarely up against the autonomies of others, and social development becomes a major phase of growth. The gifted youngster is often precocious in language development and, even at this early age, much more advanced than his peers. It is not too early to have little chats about differences in people and how important patience is in living and playing with others. Bright children may seek out adults or older youngsters as companions when age mates fail to keep pace with their more complex plans. They should be encouraged to take part in some activities with age peers in order to prevent feelings of "different" or "misfit" to warp self-perception. It is a good idea to seek out playmates of similar abilities so that the child is early aware that there are some others like him, even though they may not be the majority.

In such a way, the child is more likely to develop a liking for cooperative activities and a flexibility in sharing leadership roles even in play. Many gifted little ones show a surprising amount of self-sufficiency and an early ability to amuse and occupy themselves. They should not be pressured into group activities all of the time but should be provided with opportunities to play with similar children and also to enjoy the variable and differing abilities of age peers. Then the child learns to say "That's a good idea," as well as "This is the way we play it."

Erikson has described the psychosocial development of the three- to four-year old as a time of awareness of identity of the person as an individual with recognized traits and stability of personhood over time: "I am a girl," "I am fussy," "I am a big eater," "I don't like gooey things," "I am lovable," "I want to be just like Momma," "I'm Daddy's girl."

The child is assembling through the looking glass of parents and environment the ingredients of her image of self. In this intuitive stage of ego construction are formed the building blocks which will be searchingly scrutinized and perhaps reassembled in the later period of identity focus, adolescence. Gender identity and life role behaviors are explored in these early years. Supportive parents can help both daughters and sons to be both curious and flexible in their role play behavior in order to prevent such rigidly stereotyped attitudes as one three-year-old girl expressed too vehemently to a male classmate in the kitchen-play area of a very progressive nursery school: "You put away the mop, boys don't scrub floors!"

The preschooler is also at the stage where guilt feelings are first experienced. Erikson characterizes it as the age of *initiative vs. guilt.* Responsibility for one's acts and a sense of one's personal power to affect the environment will commonly foster a sense of accomplishment and mastery. But sometimes the child's actions are displeasing to loved ones and may even cause damage or injury. That same sense of personal responsibility which gave satisfaction may also cause unhappiness and guilt when things "go wrong." Parents should be wary of inducing guilt feelings unnecessarily or disproportionately. Guilt is probably the most painful emotion that any human being ever has to bear and self-blame is a major contributor. Parents can misuse this emotion as a tool for controlling a child's behavior when the child is shamed or made to feel instrumentally responsible for the daily mishaps which the four-year-old is heir to.

Assume a good intent in all the child's actions. Let him know that, even in a situation with distressing outcomes, you realize that he didn't intend such hurt or damage. Children so young are seldom able to take the viewpoint of others or understand another's sensibilities and often cause distress where none was intended.

With gifted children, parents may form unrealistically high expectations for maturity in social and emotional growth that would parallel the precocious rate of growth in mental development. In communicating by look, word, or action, their disappointment when the child inevitably falls short of such inappropriate expectations, parents may be adding to the burden of guilt to which the extraordinarily perceptive gifted preschooler is unhappily susceptible. It does not occur to young children to question the standards and goals set for them by the most powerful people in the world, their parents. Nor are they able to reject the parental judgment of not coming up to standard. Thus, they necessarily feel

like failures when their behavior deviates from parental expectations, even when those expectations are inappropriate.

Big dollops of praise for social accomplishments, like patience, kindness, and sharing, plus understanding of defiances and
failures will help to prevent the beginnings of the negative feelings
about self which are surprisingly prevalent in gifted school-age
children.

Researchers in Chicago (Leaverton and Herzog 1979) found
that a group of 113 highly gifted elementary school students ranked
in the bottom third of age-mates in self-acceptance and in the
bottom fourth in social confidence.

These gifted youngsters had, by then, internalized very high
standards for self through the psychodynamics of parent-child
interaction and felt that they were falling short of the mark. Early
parental awareness of the extent to which their hopes and expectations for a child become internalized by the child during this
period when his ego is not yet well enough defined for independent
judgment should make parents think hard about these hopes and
expectations. To what extent are they a projection of unfulfilled
personal dreams and goals? How much are they a reflection of the
interests and status of the parents? What seems good to the parent
is often simply assumed to be good for the child. To what extent
will the emerging interests and priorities of the child help to shape
parental encouragement? The answers to such questions help to
determine whether the child develops into the captain of his ship,
becomes a reluctant passenger, or even moves to be a stowaway on
another ship.

Gifted youngsters who feel good about themselves have parents who valued them as whole, many-faceted persons, parents
who were not blinded by the gift.

Gifted teenagers and adults frequently report their childhood
impressions that fathers and mothers responded to them chiefly as
prodigies, never seeming to know the child as a person. In their
laudable desire to provide every opportunity for the child to realize a special potential, parents should be careful to maintain a
healthy balance in their interaction with talented youngsters. Children should feel wanted for who they are rather than for what they
do. The totality of the child is valued and interesting and no single
aspect of ability should be the sole focus of reward or punishment.
If you can't be yourself in your own home, accepted and loved in

the entire spectrum of your being, then where is there a secure spot in the universe?

Others may nourish the body, foster the growth of the intellect, train the special skill, but the parent has an irreplaceable role in the development of the self-concept, the core of an individual's awareness of being. This is the fascination and challenge of parenting, and it can go forward regardless of the poverty or affluence of the family in material things. The priceless gifts of unconditional love and stable confidence are the richest heritage from the family treasure chest.

When the child reaches school age she has left behind the immature awareness of thought processes that led her to the belief that all persons in a given situation had a common consciousness parallel to the common external physical events. She learns that her thoughts are her own, hidden unless communicated and often different from the thoughts of companions or family. She discovers the joy of formulating a new idea, of finding her own solution to a problem. These are pleasurable activities for all children but often intensely so for gifted children. All of us enjoy doing what we do well.

The culture of the school now has a heavy impact on the child's self-concept. In most cases, the school environment carries an emphasis on conformity, predetermined structure, and the security of the answer the teacher has in mind. Erikson describes the years between five and eight as the period of *industry vs. inferiority.* For many children, this is the first experience of immersion in a group of peers where daily, even hourly, comparisons are made between the performances of individuals. Teacher expectations and peer pressures contribute powerful new influences on an individual's image of self as a competent person, an accepted and desirable person. The group culture shock may be experienced prior to age five when a precocious child enters nursery school settings with less-able three- and four-year olds.

Unaware of the reasons for lack of understanding in conversations and play planning attempts with age peers, gifted tots often turn to adults in the nursery school setting as the main target for interaction. It is desirable that preschool experiences for gifted children include some ability peers as well as age peers so that social interactions with like-age children are stimulating and reciprocal.

By seeking out such settings, parents can avoid the problems experienced by one highly gifted but poorly adjusting four-year-old nursery school pupil who, when asked by a psychologist who his best friends were, named only a few adult males who were actually his father's friends. A new placement in New York's Hunter College school for the gifted brought about happy changes in his social relationships when he was able to play and learn with age mates of similar ability. The striving for autonomy and individualism is balanced in human beings by a need for human communality and belonging.

No one want to feel so different from others that he or she doesn't fit in anywhere. Gifted children report a tremendous sensitivity to being made to feel weird on account of their special talents.

In the first months of schooling, parents will need to be especially watchful for indications that the youngster is experiencing difficulty in the form of rejection by teachers or classmates. This is often a time when parents find it helpful to discuss the variety of traits which are prized in human beings and the differences in levels of excellence in various traits.

It is also helpful if the parents are realistic and comfortable in recognizing their own gifts and talents. We have asked many parents of gifted youngsters if they were gifted children. The overwhelming majority indicate very quickly that they were not. This seems to be, at least in part, symptomatic of a general anti-intellectualist glorification of the ordinary which historically characterizes American culture. If the parent is not comfortable in recognizing his or her own special gifts and is diffident or evasive in discussing them, then that apparent necessity to conceal or disguise giftedness may be unwittingly transmitted to the child. Without subscribing to the "If you've got it, flaunt it!" school of behavior, some moderate course should be sought in order to help children to be comfortable with their abilities, taking a normal human pride in successful experiences and experiencing an equally normal human frustration when the challenge sometimes exceeds their efforts.

Industry in children is nurtured by mastery of new tasks and recognition by important others of the new levels of success. Parents necessarily play a pivotal role in providing appropriate support and reinforcement during the often difficult period of transition from the home environment to the school environment. Feldhusen and Wyman (1980) tell us that gifted children especially have an adaptive need to develop independence, strong self-direction, and self-discipline in learning, since schools will often fail them and they are often forced to provide for themselves.

The extreme case of one young girl illustrates the vital role her father played in her early development of a positive self-image.

Her parents noted her unique talents very early and testing indicated an IQ of 170. In the face of institutional intransigence, the father doctored the child's birth certificate in order to provide for admission to kindergarten at age four. (This author is not endorsing such a procedure.) Once there, she read her own books while older classmates struggled with the alphabet.

Other kids in ensuing classes called her a "brain" and rejected her. Teachers stopped calling on her because they knew she knew the answers. These are all-too-familiar experiences for gifted children. In later years, the high school principal told her when she won fourteen awards that she was not more able—just luckier. This is not a rare occurrence for highly gifted students. A friend's oldest son was denied several of the awards which he earned as a high school senior on the grounds that it wasn't fair for him to receive them all. One may ask, "Fair to whom?"

The young girl of our story started Princeton at 16 and one year later, in an interview focused on her schooling and relationships with teachers and age peers, reported, "I got through because my father kept telling me that I was great. That was all the strength I needed to face setbacks, like teachers who hated me."

Teachers are often uncomfortable or threatened by exceptionally able pupils, and the children may feel hated. They must have parental support. In Chapter 13 some suggestions will be offered for lessening the friction between pupil and teachers, between family and school.

When parents find that they have a gifted youngster they may feel that they have a weighty obligation to provide every opportunity for enhancing the child's special talents, and some become extremely anxious, often guilt-prone, about fulfilling that obligation. A healthy awareness of the child's unique abilities and interests is desirable. Supportiveness in response to these interests is important. But the most important contribution that parents make to the happy development of their gifted child is a secure and positive sense of self. Parents are the major factor in the shaping of self-concept and, though others may contribute in many ways to the realization of the child's abilities, the parent is the key figure in the nurturing of personhood.

Memories of childhood are built into the self-concept. In *The Brothers Karamazov*, Dostoevski expressed it thus: "there is nothing higher and stronger and more wholesome and good for life in the future than some good memory, especially a memory of childhood, of home. People talk a great deal about your education, but some good sacred memory, preserved from childhood is perhaps the best education. If a man carries such memories with him into his life, he is safe to the end of his days, and if only one good memory remains in our hearts, even that may sometime be the means of saving us."

Parents should strive to form families which work together to help every member develop these personal strengths:

1. A security that is rooted in a belief in individual worth

2. Insight into their own strengths and weaknesses as well as those of others

3. Intellectual curiosity and a willingness to take risks in exploration

4. A respect for goodness, honesty, friendliness, compassion, patience, and moral courage

5. Self-reliance and willingness to take responsibility for one's actions

6. Ability to get along with, enjoy, and help people of all ages, races, and socioeconomic and educational levels.

Parents provide excellent conditions for the nurturance of the above qualities if they demonstrate by their own behavior that:

1. They set a high value on the things they want a child to learn, morally, socially, or intellectually.

2. They time their responses sensitively to suit the individual child's needs. If a child asks a question about sex, they answer it but only tell a little more than the child had asked. They stop when the child shows boredom or lack of comprehension. They resist a temptation to unload the entire story when the child seeks only one piece of information.

3. They stress self-reliance and allow the child to handle each situation and solve each problem that lies within the child's ability, even if the parent can do it faster and better.

4. They use very little pressure in academic matters but stand ready to give help if needed or to broaden experience in an area in which the child shows an interest.

Let parents then accept children for who they are rather than what they do. What they do will grow out of who they are. Let parents provide acceptance without exploitation, understanding without prejudice, guidance without domination, and rejoice in raising a child happy with herself.

8

Equal Opportunity at Home

I NVOLVEMENT with children and their parents and teachers has enabled me to observe the sex-role behaviors of children at every age. It is surprising to find how early the effects of sex-role stereotyping can be seen in very young children's play activities as they enter nursery school or kindergarten. Clearly these stereotypes have been developed, perhaps unwittingly, at home (Moss 1967). Some teachers accept and reinforce these stereotypes; in fact, teachers have indicated to me that parents get very upset if the teacher attempts to break down sex-role patterns which dictate that boys play with the giant blocks, trucks, and move to marching music while girls play in the doll corner, clean up the work tables after pasting activities, and move to tinkly ballet music.

Although we read a great deal about some giant strides forward in breaking down traditional barriers for both men and women in acceptable roles and life styles, old ways die hard.

Sex-role stereotyping has an especially harmful impact on gifted boys and girls. To a much greater extent then their less able peers, both boys and girls combine traits traditionally attributed to their own and to the opposite sex, a concept discussed by Bem (1974) as psychological androgyny. Families and schools have not, in the past, encouraged the simultaneous development of "masculine" and "feminine" traits within a single person.

The traditional definition of masculinity includes such characteristics as independence and assertiveness. To be feminine includes interpersonal sensitivity, dependence, and nurturance.

Those who study productively creative people find that highly creative males appear to be "feminine" and sensitive while highly creative females appear to be "masculine" and independent. These traits have been assessed on traditional personality measures with a stereotypic continuum on the masculinity-femininity dimension. (Two typical items from interest scales might be noted: to express a preference for outdoor activities scores as masculine, to prefer reading as a leisure activity scores as feminine.)

Encouragement for both men and women to combine "masculine" and "feminine" traits, to be more fully human, expands the range of roles and behaviors open to every person.

Adults of both sexes who have been able to combine both aspects to become psychologically androgynous show above-average levels of self-esteem and a strong sense of ego identity. They feel that they have a greater potential for functioning as full human beings. They value openness, flexibility, and self-reliance, and they have low concern for social norms.

Few people would argue about the desirability of these traits and values in the abstract, but in daily living with our own sons and daughters, social and family relations regarding sex-role appropriate behaviors and attitudes have a much more concrete impact.

In 1949 the noted anthropologist Margaret Mead wrote about the double-bind of expectations for boys and girls. The boy is taught to achieve; the girl to show that she does not achieve, will never achieve. According to Mead, a parallel threat hung over the under-achieving boy and the achieving girl. Neither would ever be chosen by a member of the opposite sex.

In 1986, despite educational and legislative changes, much the same holds true in the area of interpersonal relationships. A recent newspaper article described the failure of marriages where the wife made more money, had a more responsible position than the husband, or was employed in a non-traditional job. In many instances, the effects were so painful to the men and to their self-esteem that the love relationship could not survive. Such surveys convey a powerful and sad message to gifted boys and girls who seek to pursue non-traditional paths. A more secure sense of self and individual values could often forestall such unhappiness. These are personal strengths which are best enhanced by supportive parents who themselves avoid stereotypes in their expectations for and responses to each child, whether male or female.

Our society has historically exercised many restraints to the full development of gifted girls in the pursuit of a fulfilling career.

Gifted young women still often find themselves in a no-win situation as they try to reconcile their personal interests and educational preparation with the areas of excellence socially approved for females. The stereotypic feminine virtues are seriously at odds with career advancement.

Submissiveness is still expected from women. At the very least, she should be non-assertive; heaven forbid that she should be aggressive. Yet ambitious, aggressive behavior in men is seen as desirable and leads to advancement.

Physical attractiveness and some erotic qualities are prized in women. Young girls are often encouraged to cultivate these attributes, yet such factors are widely perceived as unprofessional in women while they do not detract from the career success of men.

Women possess the hands that rock the cradle, are expected to be nurturant, and to place home responsibilities above the job. Men who exhibit such a value system would not go far in their careers. Women who do prefer professional life to a family life are widely perceived as aberrant and unfeminine. It is true that a small but growing number of enlightened employers are providing flexible work hours which permit women to combine careers and families.

In today's world, the gifted woman still battles traditional attitudes. If she succeeds as a wife, mother, and professional, she must be letting down in at least one area. Rather than flourishing in her multi-dimensional accomplishments, she is continuously defending against stereotypic social perceptions.

Young women who are succeeding at this balancing act usually attribute much of their strength and perseverance in nontraditional goals to a very supportive father who encouraged them to be fully themselves and who told them often that they could be whatever they wanted to be.

Parental support in the upstream battle against pressures to conform are important for gifted youngsters of both sexes. However, Schwartz (1980) listed several reasons why it is more complex and more needed in the case of gifted girls. She described the dichotomy in expectations for "Gifted Students" and "Females."

Gifted students are expected to develop their individual talents to the fullest. Females are expected to be nurturant, selfless, and giving.

Gifted students should be active, exploring and self-assertive. Females are reinforced for passive and dependent behaviors.

Gifted students should prepare for a challenging career. Females prepare to maintain a well-run household.

Gifted students are urged to "realize one's own potential." Females are taught to put husband's career first. Often their mothers are significant models of that practice and fathers who benefit seldom contradict in either word or action.

All of us are shaped by the society we live in, and many parents contribute to the role confusion of gifted daughters. Parents need the strength to be non-conformists, too, in their encouragement of freedom to grow and to excel for their daughters as well as their sons.

It should be helpful to parents, especially fathers, to be aware of the reasons for not reaching the top which gifted young women reported to Horner (1973) in her widely noted study of female fear of success. Sensitivity to these feelings which are common to gifted girls will assist parents in lessening the inhibiting impact on their own daughters' aspirations.

The most widely cited fear was of male resentment of female leadership and excellence. This shows itself very early in the observed regression in female achievement at the age when interest in the opposite sex emerges. Significant decrements in girls' achievement are noted at the middle school or junior high.

The second factor reported in Horner's study was family responsibilities. (Every career person needs a housebody.)

Mothers and fathers should examine the patterns which are being established in the home. In many instances, daughters are expected to make a much larger contribution to household maintenance than are the sons. A boy's schooling, extracurricular activities, or part-time work often are treated by the whole family as his first priority, reducing obligations at home. The girl is usually expected to carry out a significant share of chores in addition to schooling, perhaps in priority over extracurricular involvements, and she is much less likely as an adolescent to be gainfully employed outside her home.

Girls can rake leaves, boys can clean the kitchen. Genuine equity should be sought in both the nature of and time spent in family chores. Such equity in children's assignments is underscored by similar parental sharing of family responsibilities. Our children are much more impressed by what we do than what we say.

A word here about voluntarism is appropriate. The overwhelming preponderance of women in society's unpaid roles also sends a powerful message to females that they are expected to be giving and nurturant and nobly unremunerated financially. Few males have the time or inclination for these worthy activities. The message frequently internalized is that women's time is not as important as men's.

A third factor in female fear of success, according to Horner's subjects, was lack of confidence. This finding is also supported in the work of Fleming and Hollinger (1979) in which a large group of girls from a broad spectrum of economic and cultural backgrounds showed irrationally low levels of self-evaluation and career aspirations considering their exceptional demonstrated abilities. Families play a central role in the image of self which children acquire. Families also contribute in large part to the career expectancies of their youngsters. When parents are sensitized to the pervasive lack of confidence found in gifted daughters, they will surely seek out ways to bring self-evaluation into congruence with high potential and to promote realistic aspirations for productive high-level careers in fields of choice.

A fourth drawback to the professional advancement of gifted females is the lack of shared experience. There are few female role models at the top in many fields. Mentors of the same sex are rarely available as a woman moves up the career ladder. She usually finds herself more and more in the company of men. This has proven to make both professional and personal life very lonely for women in non-traditional careers. Rosalyn Yalow, the woman physicist and Nobel prize winner, who narrated the PBS television series on the life of fellow Nobel prize winner Marie Curie, commented most tellingly on this aspect of Madame Curie's life following the death of her scientist husband. Dr. Yalow frankly described her own personal sense of alone-ness and exclusion from the professional give-and-take, the day-to-day sharing of ideas, which was regularly enjoyed by her male colleagues. The early death of Rosalind Franklin, the female researcher who contributed significantly to Watson and Crick's vaunted discovery of the double helix of DNA, has been attributed to a near total lack of recognition of her part in that work. Who remembers her name at all? Or that of Jocelyn Bell, whose work on black holes seems to have fallen into one? This is not very encouraging for would-be female scientists. The drive and the ego must be exceedingly strong to overcome such negative images.

One of the serendipitous outcomes of the Project Choice program (Fleming and Hollinger 1979) was the coming together of many career women who agreed to function as models and mentors for the gifted girls in the program. These women delighted in each other and relished the rare opportunity to share experiences. They also welcomed the opportunity to foster the development of the gifted schoolgirls who wanted to explore career alternatives. Parents of gifted girls and boys should seek out same-sex role models for their children in careers of interest to the youngsters of either sex, at any socioeconomic level.

The foregoing factors probably contribute to the Horner subjects' reported lack of interest in moving up. The young women wished to avoid the competition and stress that appear to accompany executive responsibility. They did not want to be like the men they saw in those roles and had few female models or guides to provide more positive reinforcement.

The remaining factor in fear of success is lack of an appropriate education. Aware parents can take an active part in counteracting well-meaning stereotyping by both male and female school counselors who too often provide inappropriate academic scheduling for gifted girls, and teachers or coaches who consciously or unconsciously reinforce time-worn stereotypes about what girls should be good at versus what boys should be good at. Educators should foster equal psychological opportunity as well as equal legal access. Parents should insist on this during the formative early years in which the groundwork for adult aspirations is laid down.

Those women who were professionally excelling reported as positive factors: (a) strong support from parents, especially *fathers*, (b) relish for the challenge, "women have to be twice as competent as men to get half as far," (c) successful female role models, and (d) their own experience that female excellence does not necessarily destroy social life.

The gifted boy who exhibits such stereotypically feminine traits as nurturance, sensitivity, passivity is also victimized by parental or social rejection of those aspects of his personhood. The father is obviously well pleased by the son who wants to be an engineer but mystified and disappointed by the son who wants to be a novelist. A caring and protective mother may smuggle a high school boy's tights and ballet shoes out of the house for a little theater audition, but the father's inability to accept such ambitions in a son carries a powerful message to a multitalented young man. Seeing the son of a U.S. president in the ballet may have helped to break down the stereotypes; media attention to his heterosexual living arrangements before his marriage was also palliative.

Adult males whose nurturant or artistic tendencies have been inhibited in their expression by social and family disapprobation find present support in male consciousness-raising groups. These are fewer in number than similar female-oriented groups but they can be found in many communities. The need for such groups points up the fact that stereotyping of sex-appropriate traits and behaviors has severe psychological impacts on men as well as women.

The upsurge of the feminist movement and the more intense need to redress socioeconomic imbalances has generated a much more visible body of literature about the negative pressures on gifted females.

Related studies of expressive characteristics and the male psyche would probably contribute much to our understanding and parenting of gifted boys. Certainly parental pressures to achieve are much higher on boys than on girls and career choices, although more diverse, are still stereotyped.

I remember my own surprise in our supposedly enlightened household when my teen-age daughters expressed concern over their younger brother's delight in creative stitchery and his desire to learn to knit. I could prevent their making negative comments to him but his own peers soon succeeded in squelching those "girl's" interests. Only a few of his childish creations survive.

The same girls were very quick to comment if their brother did not get equal time at the sink or stove. Does parity mean equal shares of only the undesirable activities, not extending to the enjoyable aesthetic pastimes?

Mothers and fathers can provide powerful non-sexist models in the ways that they share professional and home-making roles and in the equality with which they respond to both daughters and sons. In that wonderful pre-feminist movement book, *Cheaper by the Dozen* (1948) Lillian Gilbreth's children described a successful two-career family. She taught that (a) developing together a written list of necessities, (b) setting priorities, and (c) trying hard to maintain a schedule would enrich parenting for both mother and father. When routine matters are under control and not permitted to swallow up all of either parent's home time, then a mother can more flexibly respond to the needs of an individual child and also have some time to herself, while the father will be able to experience many more of the intimacies, the challenges, and joys of parenting.

Dr. Gilbreth's outstanding talents as a time-study consultant—as well as those of her husband—surely contributed much to the successful rearing of twelve children. I believe it is timely to note here that, in her study of families of gifted children in England, Freeman (1979) found that the mothers of the most stable school-age children were most likely to work outside the home. In an earlier study in which most mothers were employed outside the home, Ferri (1976) concluded that the behavioral and educational handicaps sometimes suffered by children in one-parent families are more likely to be caused by poverty, poor housing, or ethnic discrimination than with specific absence of a male or female parental role model.

Encouragement of desirable "masculine" and "feminine" traits within the same individual, independence and sensitivity, assertiveness and understanding, will develop a person with greater potential for functioning at full human capacity. Such an androgynous gifted youngster in our present sex-stereotyped society will need parental support in order to remain open to all experiences, flexible, accepting of ambiguities, undaunted by social conventions and sturdily self-reliant—a flourishing human being.

9

The Early Years

D URING the planning session in a school system newly embark-
ing on a program for educating gifted youngsters, one of the
elementary principals who had investigated such programs in sur-
rounding school districts jokingly said, "They don't get gifted until
the fourth grade." This tongue-in-cheek comment reflects an all-
too-general neglect of the needs of preschool and primary age
gifted and talented children. Any survey of public school programs
in the education of the gifted gives evidence of a lack of special
provisions for the exceptionally able young child (Wilkie 1985).
Fewer than 10 percent of the school systems in this area currently
offer programming for gifted children which includes kindergarten or first and second grades. The most common starting level
is third or fourth grade. Despite the increase of published concern
for early childhood education, a questionnaire circulated among
university faculty responsible for teacher preparation for gifted
and talented education in one state showed the lowest priority
being given to programming for the preschool/primary child.

This is a matter of deep concern for educators and developmental psychologists whose experience and training have focused
on the young child and who have seen first hand the psychological
damage and waste that frequently result when the appropriate
intellectual stimulation and psychoeducational support are not
provided for our most able during those vulnerable early years
(Whitmore 1980). Parents of very young gifted children give continuous witness to the problem as they seek the help of external
consultants in meeting the needs of their special children. Many

anxious parents hark back to their own early memories of boredom, frustration, and pain in their earliest school years and seek to prevent similar experiences for their youngsters.

In my own experiences supervising student teachers in kindergarten and primary classrooms, I have been struck again and again by observing the occurrence of the acting-out, "disruptive" boy or girl, about whom the teacher was most likely to say, "I just don't know what to do with him, I've tried everything—and those test scores in his folder are certainly not accurate—130 IQ!—he sure doesn't show it in here." Such repeated similar events brought me to the point of suggesting a new approach to early identification. These experiences certainly provide empathy for parents and children caught in such situations. Needless to report, the teachers were not too happy either, and would do better if they knew how.

The widely expressed attitude that gifted children have a greater number of abilities and coping mechanisms and thus can make it on their own is especially harmful with respect to children in these intensively formative years. Many writers have stressed the critical nature of the years between two and seven in affecting an individual's psychosocial and cognitive development. Hunt (1961), Piaget (1955, 1962), Bloom (1964), and Schaeffer (1980) stress the importance of the environment in providing the appropriate match in order to foster optimum growth. McCarthy (1980), in a much-needed collection on educating the very young child, includes the suggestion that school beginning time may be the most stressful period of adjustment that gifted children encounter, a time of greatest dysynchrony between phases of development (Perez 1980). As David Feldman (1979) has stated, the remarkable feats of highly gifted children have not been achieved in the absence of intense, prolonged, educational assistance.

During these years from two to seven, the child moves from the stage which Erikson (1963) describes as personal autonomy through the stage of personal initiative toward the stage of industry, while refining a sense of identity and learning what aspects of the individual, other than his or her own wish to learn, affect the learning environment. Such aspects will include sex, skin color, speech patterns, clothing, and evidence of ability. This period could be thought of as "childescence," a time of transition from infant dependency to child competency. In a sense, the reorganization of the emerging personality is analogous to the more familiar identity crisis of adolescence. For the young child, this is a period of ambivalence between the urges of the id-oriented, exuberant pleasure in growth versus the more mature, adult-oriented murmurings of the developing superego, which support and increase self-observation, self-guidance, and self-punishment. It is during these years that the perfectionism which can be so debilitating to gifted children may take root (Whitmore 1980). Parent and teacher understanding and support are crucial here.

Especially in these years of emerging initiative and industry, the child is more ready to learn quickly and avidly, to become "bigger" in the sense of sharing both responsibilities and activities. The child is eager and able to make things cooperatively, to join with others for purposes of planning and constructing, gaining feelings of effectancy (White 1959). The child is willing to profit from teachers and to emulate prototypes. Helpful models with whom the gifted child can identify can have tremendous impact at this time.

As Erikson has so eloquently told us, these early stages (initiative and industry) set the direction toward the possible and the tangible which permit the dreams and fantasies of early childhood to be attached to the goals of an active and productive adult life.

What makes this transitition from private world to public world so potentially traumatic for gifted and talented young children? It is not the fact that they are so bright that creates the difficulty, but the fact that they are different. These differences become most apparent to the child upon immersion in the large group culture of the schools. Parents and teachers can be most helpful during these vulnerable years if they are aware of and sensitive to these differences and can talk about them with the child, helping him or her to understand that uniqueness.

These differences have been described earlier in the overlapping categories of advanced cognitive development, psychosocial sensitivity, and physical characteristics and are briefly reviewed here.

ADVANCED COGNITIVE DEVELOPMENT

1. With broad perceptual sensitivity, they take in everything in the environment and have tremendous curiosity about how things work, why things are, what if conditions were

changed. They have the ability to attend to several things at one time, along with a need to explore the environment actively.

2. They have the ability to see relationships and to make inferences about causality and function; they like systems and they like to fantasize alternative systems.

3. Excellent memory assisted by early language abilities and ability to classify and categorize help develop storage strategies which greatly enhance retrieval.

4. Children exhibit extensive vocabulary, with frequently more denotative, not always connotative, meanings for their words (many gifted children love to read dictionaries but lack the experiential references of more mature speakers), and they often make up words.

5. Along with the ability to tolerate cognitive ambiguity, resist early closure, and enjoy complex tasks and open-ended tasks, gifted children hate to be told the answer.

6. Some have advanced mathematical skills in both computation and reasoning, interests which may suppress reading precocity.

7. Children have an extended concentration span and task persistence.

8. Intensity of task involvement and a lack of the foresight and prudence which come with experience lead them often to bite off more than they can chew. They need adult understanding and moderating guidance but they *should* try sometimes and fail.

PSYCHOSOCIAL SENSITIVITY

1. They reveal a sense of justice and what is fair; advanced moral development follows on advanced cognitive development.

2. Children share a value system with a broad compass, perceive injustices in the larger society, set high standards for self and others, respond to truth, justice, harmony, and nature.

3. Vivid imagining, playfulness in work, creativity, inventiveness (imaginary friends, siblings, rich fantasy life) are frequent traits.

4. These children have a great sense of humor, love incongruities, puns, and pranks, and often see things as funny when peers do not.

5. They are easily frustrated, still young children, dependent, impatient, intense, lacking in emotional balance.

6. They sometimes have exaggerated fears and are exceptionally sensitive to the nonverbal signs of those about them, high vulnerability.

7. Egocentrism is normal at this age.

8. They often have a negative self-concept and low social acceptance with age peers.

PHYSICAL CHARACTERISTICS

1. With a high energy level, they often need less than normal amounts of sleep, no naps.

2. Their fine motor coordination and manual dexterity are often not as advanced as cognition; they need practice opportunities and can become frustrated and exhibit dependency behaviors.

3. Their eyes are often not mature (prior to age 8), especially with respect to changing of focus from near to far (desk to chalkboard).

Consideration of the ways in which gifted and talented preschool and primary age children most often differ from their age peers can guide parents and teachers in both nurturing and challenging the totality of development in each fascinating individual.

In the cognitive area, the following suggestions have been most well received by concerned parents.

Listen carefully to the children's questions, *observe voluntary activities, and follow the child's natural interests.* If a five-year-old with an IQ somewhere in the area of 200 (off the scale) shows no interest in learning to read but multiplies three digits by three digits rapidly in his head, don't drill him in the alphabet. It is sometimes difficult for parents with strong talents and interests to permit the child not to share them. Encourage the child to explain his or her interests to you and ask honest questions about those areas of interest. Even though you yourself may not be an expert resource on the topic, your questions often help to give some direction. When parental limits of expertise are reached, urge the child to write to experts. Seek out interests that can be shared and let your interaction in some selected area be a long-term plan in which you can become a learner, too.

Answer those myriad questions. Our gifted three and four-year-olds are highly curious and anxious to explore all aspects of the environment. They persist longer than the average youngster does. It is important to answer with patience, good humor, and respect. Take advantage of questions to encourage the child into further learning and explorations. The worst response parents can make is, "You ask too many questions!" The mother of one fortunate gifted boy would greet him on his return from school, not with, "What did you learn today?" but "What questions did you ask today?"

Do not emphasize school-type activities just because materials are commercially available and easy for the child. Such activities usually focus heavily on convergent rather than divergent thinking and narrow the child's thinking rather than broadening it. There is growing attention being given to right and left brain hemisphere-related mental functions. Traditional school activities tend to unduly emphasize the logical, digital, linear processes associated with left hemisphere dominance. The intuitive, relational thinking which Piaget (1962) tells us is natural in the preschool child may be stifled by early, heavy involvement with the structured, workbook-type materials so widely advertised and easily available.

Activities which very young gifted children have frequently enjoyed include keeping a journal, writing and illustrating a newspaper, compiling the family genealogy with accompanying photographs and oral histories, making family samplers or quilts, analyzing the family budget for a year, using a microscope to examine the flora and fauna of the neighborhood, and maintaining collections of all kinds.

A wide range of interests should be encouraged. Physical and social activities both with other gifted children and with heterogeneous peer groups are desirable. Cultivate enjoyment of activity for its own sake rather than as an opportunity to excel.

Japanese preschoolers have intensive movement and music, drama, and group cooperative activities. This seems more in keeping with Piagetian theory positing the need to lay a rich experiential base on which to build more mature cognitive functioning and involves all areas of the brain (Torrance 1979).

Provide private space and storage facilities for collections, hobbies and experiments. Classifying, categorizing, recognizing systems, and seeing relationships are intellectually satisfying activities for gifted children. These activities are readily engaged in by many forms of nature study (even in a city backyard) or basic physical science and mechanics. The homely hobby of gardening offers applications from chemistry, language (Latin names for all the plants), planning continual production for a balanced diet or aesthetic pleasure in continuous flowering and color combinations, entomology, and economics. The work involved also reinforces industry and the enjoyment of the product of one's efforts.

Adapt the mentor model for preschool activities sponsored by parent groups. What special talents do moms and dads have? What weekend morning or week-day groups can be formed (in lieu of often-resisted naps)? Parents might pool funds and hire a foreign language teacher for an interested set of preschoolers, capitalizing on the gifted child's playfulness with language and optimum flexibility of the language acquisition centers of the brain.

Activities promoting group discussions are also good, as these opportunities to clarify thoughts and test ideas are excellent for intellectual development and allow children to experience the differing perceptions and thoughts of their peers.

In the psychosocial domain the parents' most vital obligation to their gifted offspring is to let them know that they are *valued for themselves,* in all aspects of their being, rather than for their special area of giftedness.

It is often very difficult for parents and teachers to accept that the majority of gifted children have negative self-concepts (Rowlands 1974). This is, in part, a consequence of the perfectionism which plagues many of our highly gifted children. How do these children come to set such high standards for themselves? What parental expectations are being communicated? Is being best what earns parental attention? How much projection of their unrealized hopes and dreams are parents consciously or unconsciously putting on these children? Parents and teachers should avoid the halo effect, expecting excellence in everything. Be sure that the child is exposed *early* to activities in which he or she may not excel. One can do and enjoy activities in which one is not the best. One does not always succeed. Lack of success in some areas is all right, part of living, and accepted by all.

Parents can respond to the reduced need for sleep in gifted children by encouraging restful activities rather than naps. Some will read, listen to tapes of parents reading favorite stories, or work at jigsaw puzzles when they resist sleeping during the day. Their motors usually run in such high gear that they need some idling times—and so do parents.

Primary emphasis in this discussion has been given to the responsibility and privilege of parents in the education of the young gifted child. At present, schools are generally a long way from adequate programming at preschool or primary level. It is to be hoped that educational provisions will improve in the future, but even when and if they do, the parents will remain the major resource and support of their gifted children. A blessed challenge ! The prognosis is good when parents provide intelligent educational options, consistent guidance, and emotional support.

PART III
Cherishing

Stimulation and Challenge

A COMMENT I often hear from parents is, "I don't want my child to be a genius—just let him be a normal, well-adjusted happy child." Such a statement gives rise to many questions. Much negative stereotyping forms the basis of that attitude in the families of highly gifted children. In fact, it is just this type of parental verbalization that gave major impetus to the writing of this little book, in the hope that the primary benefactor will be the children.

Let us look first at the questions that spring to mind (and sometimes to mouth) when I hear this common parental wish expressed.

What does "normal" mean for a gifted child? In the genes with which the child was born, nourished by the environment in which he or she developed, are the biochemical bases of the wonderful traits and talents which are emerging. It is *normal* behavior for the gifted toddler to be highly curious, energetic, sensitive, quick-witted, remembering everything, and usually precociously verbal and independent. These are not *average* behaviors in their age-level peers, but they are *normal* behaviors for bright children. Do parents wish their children to suppress their normal responses to the world around them, to stunt and somehow inhibit the developmental pace which their DNA is charting? Do parents truly wish their children to be other than their genuine selves? They will say that they want to save the child the heartache and alienation that is often the lot of the highly gifted in today's society. But such attitudes feed into the continuation of the stereotype that to be gifted is to be weird and rejected by one's peers. How does the child feel who hears such comments from parents or intuits their attitude from less direct responses to his or her uniqueness? "My parents are not pleased with how I am or who I am. They would like me to be more ordinary, to cover my true self." Such feelings can only have negative impact on self-concept and intensify the gifted child's sense of alienation.

How much more desirable to rejoice in the richness of the unique biochemistry of which the parents are the progenitors and to enjoy with the child the potential which unfolds. That attitude should lessen the impact of the feared social stereotypes and in time, begin to weaken negative views of our gifted youngsters.

"I wouldn't want to be as smart as Tom—to have to carry the burden of that brain all my life," said a favorite uncle in the presence of one of the most intelligent young men I have ever known. When your cherished role models, the significant others in your life, talk that way, they are unwittingly contributing to the "burden." Why should family members intensify the negative view, especially when they are usually gifted themselves as this uncle is, by paying lip service to this country's pervasive anti-intellectualism and near idolatry of the "common man"?

We also give lip-service to the value of the individual and the open door of opportunity. Let us then rather cherish the superior potential that some children evidence and seek to stimulate and challenge all of their abilities rather than dull them or veil them in well-meant but somehow misguided pointing to the average. We want them to be *normal* in being truly themselves.

Thus, it seems a contradiction for the parent in the same breath to wish the child to be well-adjusted and happy. It is hard to be well-adjusted when all the burden for adjusting falls on the child. "Don't use such big words." "Don't ask so many questions." "Don't contradict people." "Don't show off." "Girls are not supposed to beat boys." "Wait until others are ready." "Don't work ahead." "Try not to correct the teacher." Just a few of the admonitions too often deluging the brightest children. It must seem a litany of advice urging them to adjust to the needs and sensitivities of others. Certainly, some of it is necessary and should be lovingly used by parents to foster good social relationships with people of widely varying abilities. But does the gifted child have to do all the adjusting? Can the schools, the community, the society develop more understanding and less resentment? Surely the family can be mutual in the adjusting of behaviors and attitudes. Home is the only place where any individual can expect to experience unconditional love for the true self and parents are the indispensable source of that love and security. It is within parental power to have their children well-adjusted and happy by giving total acceptance of the unique nature of each child and warm sharing in both trials and triumphs. It should also be emphasized here that self-adjustment is primary. There has been earlier discussion of the child's discovery of his or her special abilities. Being comfortable in one's own skin is easier to accomplish when those dear to you are comfortable with you and let you know in many ways that you are respected and cherished in all your being.

While mulling over final revisions of this section, I came upon the following paragraph which introduced an article on parenting gifted youngsters, "Someone once said that gifted children can be difficult to teach, hard to live with, but IMPOSSIBLE to raise" (Johnson and Roth 1985). This explicitly expresses the attitudes and feelings which this book is intended to ameliorate, if not eradicate.

Why do parents feel this way, what are the factors in family interactions and relationships which contribute to this too widely held parental response? What are the social and professional contributions which promote and perpetuate this stereotypic view of raising gifted children? Would social conventions, equally sanction a parallel statement that, "Children can be difficult to teach, hard to live with, but IMPOSSIBLE to raise?" Probably, "Yes," to the first two phrases, but not the third.

Does the third phrase have a hyperbolic function similar to, "I just washed my hair and I can't do a thing with it?" Is it really acceptable to say that a given category of children is IMPOSSIBLE in the realm of such an important shaper of personhood as child-rearing? Even if such a comment is not meant to be taken literally, what impact does it have on other parents, and on the inevitable overhearers, the children themselves? Will it not function as a self-fulfilling prophecy, weakening parents' confidence in their appropriate roles, justifying their occasional shortcomings, and exacerbating the negative influences on the developing self-concept of the sensitive youngster?

It is my hope that we can replace IMPOSSIBLE with CHALLENGING, EXHILIRATING, REWARDING and FUN!

In order to do that, it is only fair to examine some of the possible causes for the stereotypic statement. What are those challenges which contribute to frustration and disappointment in some family constellations?

It often seems that adolescence, which is frequently a period of "sturm und drang" in American culture, is a time of intensified strain in the relationships of parents to their gifted youngsters. The earlier described condition of dyssynchrony, an apparent imbalance among various phases of personal development (for example, intellectual, physical, social, emotional, moral) is again relevant here.

In discussing younger children, we have noted that with our population of interest, intellectual development is often quite accelerated, while physiological and emotional development are much more age-typical. Moral development, with its connectedness to intellectual understanding and nourishment by heightened sensitivity, is often seen to be advanced in relation to age peers. With intellectual and moral development outpacing emotional and physiological development in relationship to peer norms, it can easily be seen that social development will be under tension.

Parents begin to respond to these emerging tensions with some of the strategies described in the chapter on responding to problem behaviors. We have noted that many of these tensions become apparent first in sibling relationships when there is wide variance in the distribution of abilities within the family constellation; second, upon school entrance when peer comparisons are heightened and teacher behaviors have tremendous impact. We should also note that these tensions again cause increases in stress during the transformation from childhood to young adulthood, which the American culture extends for so many years, imposing sometimes artificial and unnecessary dependency on our young people.

It would also be helpful to consider what makes a bright child happy. The same things that make all children happy. New problems to solve, new avenues to explore, new sensations to experience—stimulation and challenge.

For most children, the nation's schools have the resources and commitment to provide sufficient stimulation and challenge to foster healthy mental, social, and physical development. Parent pressure and legislative consciences have mandated differentiated stimulus and challenge for the less able. For our most able children, the schools in general have fewer resources and, in many instances, a limited commitment to optimal educational responses for the gifted and talented. The reality, if not the equity, of our present situation is that parents will have a large responsibility in the stimulation and challenge for mental and social growth of their gifted children. It is, in large measure, due to parents' perception of this responsibility that many of those who call for advice feel inadequate, frustrated, and anxious. Often, the formal school identification process and attachment of the label is frightening to parents. In other cases, their own perceptivity has enabled them to recognize in the preschool years the unique potential of their toddlers. In many cases, they have been concerned, even overwhelmed, by their responsibility in rearing an exceptionally bright child.

Their concern is justified because they are and will continue to be a major resource in nurturing the balanced intellectual and social growth of their children. But such concern should foster an excitement in the challenge rather than fear of failure in the responsibility.

No one knows this wonderful child better than his or her family members. In planning to supplement the traditional educational opportunities of schooling, the parents should look first to the child's own interests and preferred activities. The parents should then look at the common developmental interests of children of similar ages. The evidence that a preschooler is intellectually able to perform academic tasks in language and arithmetic skills does not indicate that parents should hasten to involve their children in school-like activities such as those workbooks offered ubiquitously in supermarkets and discount stores. Children will be overexposed to these things soon enough.

Encourage and participate if possible in activities that broaden the child's base of experience in every sensory and kinesthetic dimension. This is not only fun for every one but actually provides a much richer foundation for future academic experiences.

All children are interested in the natural sciences of plants, animals, and the mineral kingdom. The earth provides almost endless resources for the gifted youngster's typical interest in collecting, categorizing, and classifying, whose delight in discovering or devising patterns is a widely noted characteristic.

The reading interests of most gifted children are voracious and although they are often capable of comprehending advanced material, their interests are often more age related than ability related and they devour the same Hardy Boys and Nancy Drew series that most young readers enjoy. They often seek out specialized and challenging books in their areas of special interest. The library is an indispensable resource for gifted children and their parents. Computer terminals and interlibrary loan systems have enhanced the availability of materials to smaller community libraries.

In books, nature, and hobby or work areas, our able youngsters need both opportunities to explore and experiment and to develop good work habits. They need practice and reinforcement for carrying a task begun through to its completion and in exercising some selectivity in the projects they begin. Of course, there must be flexibility in adult efforts to engender prudence and practicality. It is not at all uncommon for a gifted youngster to be more or less actively reading ten or twelve books concurrently. The multitude of things which interest them makes it very difficult to narrow choices to the few that they realistically have time and energy to explore at any given point in time.

It is true that their energy and intensity of interest often exceed that of less gifted enthusiasts, but they are only human and should learn not to set themselves up for frustration by continually biting off more than even Gargantua could chew.

Highly gifted children have an adaptive need to develop independence, strong self-direction, and self-discipline in learning since schools will often fail to provide adequate challenge and they need to become self-reliant, self-starters in pursuing excellence.

In school settings where little or no consideration is given to exceptional talents we find gifted children variously functioning at one of Maslow's (1954) four levels.

At the survival level, the youngster is physically present and struggling for self-maintenance. Tremendous psychological energy is tied up in the effort for preservation of self in a seemingly hostile environment. At the defending level, the youngster is maintaining a sense of self and has established a personal niche of security, but much energy is devoted to holding that ground and repelling perceived threats.

At the coping level, the gifted youngster has worked out some compromises with social and institutional constraints or rebuffs and, although some energy must be channeled into accommodation or suppression, an acceptable amount can be devoted to personal priorities for growth and learning.

The fourth level, flourishing, is our aim for gifted children and their families. In this personal psychological climate, the individual is free to devote nearly all of her energies to productive, satisfying activities (after the dishes are done and the lawn is mowed, etc.).

David Lewis (1979) has compiled a list of questions for parents which was excerpted in the *Gifted Child Newsletter* (1981). These are culled from descriptions of child-rearing practices reported by thousands of parents. They are described as typifying a successful approach to encouraging favorable mental development.

1. I answer all questions from my child as patiently and honestly as possible.

2. I take serious questions or statements from my child seriously.

3. I provide a display board where my child can show off his or her work.

4. I am prepared to tolerate an untidy work area if my child has not yet completed some creative task such as painting or model making.

5. I provide my child with a room, or part of a room, exclusively for his or her own use.

6. I show my child he or she is loved for his or her own sake, not because of achievements.

7. I give my child suitable responsibilities.

8. I help my child make his or her own plans and decisions.

9. I take my child on trips to places of interest.

10. I teach my child how to improve on the tasks he or she does.

11. I encourage my child to get along with children from different backgrounds.

12. I set a reasonable standard of behavior and see that my child follows it.

13. I never compare my child unfavorably with other children.

14. I never denigrate my child as a form of punishment.

15. I provide hobby materials and books.

16. I encourage my child to think things out for himself or herself.

17. I read regularly to my child.

18. I teach my child early reading habits.

19. I encourage my child to invent stories and fantasies.

20. I give careful consideration to the individual needs of each child.

21. I provide a time each day when my child can be alone with me.

22. I allow my child to have a say in planning family programs and trips.

23. I never mock my child for making a mistake.

24. I encourage my child to remember stories, poems, and songs.

25. I encourage my child to be sociable with adults of all ages.

26. I devise practical experiments to help my child find out about things.

27. I allow my child to play with all kinds of junk objects.

28. I encourage my child to look for problems and then solve them.

29. I look for specific things to praise in my child's activities.

30. I avoid general praise that I do not really mean.

31. I am honest about my emotions with my child.

32. I do not have any subjects that I would totally refuse to discuss with my child.

33. I provide opportunities for real decision making by my child.

34. I encourage my child to be an individual.

35. I help my child find worthwhile programs on TV.

36. I encourage my child to think positively about his or her abilities.

37. I never dismiss failures by my child with the comment, "I can't do it either!"

38. I encourage my child to be as independent of adults as possible.

39. I have faith in my child's good sense and I trust him or her.

40. I would sooner my child failed by himself or herself than succeeded because I did most of the work.

I find it helpful to share this checklist with parents and then to discuss the number of "yes" responses they were able to make. If one could agree to twenty or fewer of the statements, then maybe some of the neglected activities are worth exploring. But if parents agree to 90 percent or more, then perhaps they ought to back off and give both the children and themselves more breathing room. We must keep a prudent balance between supporting healthy growth and hothouse forcing. Our gifted children are first of all children. It seems that this can not be reiterated enough, and I think that this intuitive realization is at the heart of the parental comment with which this chapter began. I believe firmly that parents, teachers, and children strive always for what they believe to be best. Lack of successful outcomes is due not to failure of intent but to lack of insight or experience.

In the effort then to reduce anxiety and increase joy in parenting, let me suggest that parents should first *accept* realistically the necessity for going beyond the school's resources and providing appropriate stimulation and challenge for their children.

Secondly, parents should become knowledgeable about child development through reading and interaction with other interested parents and professionals. Many universities offer courses of interest and have extensive library resources. There are frequently local parent groups. There are national organizations with publications of interest to both parents and children. The appendixes to this book include a bibliography and list of national organizations.

Third, the parents should spend a week or so in observation, listening, and mental or actual note-taking, focusing on the child's interests and daily activities. This will provide strong clues about directions in which time and energy will most happily be invested. Let the child's curiosity be your guide in providing stimulation and challenge. A daily journal may also expose some cases of over-scheduling, with the child's days so full of structured activities that there is little time for reflection or improvisation. If that should be the case, maybe parents will want to re-examine the impetus for participation in each area. The deepest need of children is to be pleasing to and loved by their parents and they will often participate in an activity because they know it makes their parents happy or proud and that is sufficient reason for doing it. Parents may want to consider the child's need for some truly free time. Daydreaming or "hanging-out" can be healthy changes of pace.

Fourth, as general guidelines in cherishing their children through stimulation and challenge, parents should consider three factors which have been found to contribute to superior performance. In addition to early recognition of potential, these are *capacity*, *opportunity*, and *personality*.

The *capacity* for acute perception, abstract and complex thinking, verbal or mathematical fluency, or artistic expression is among the attributes that cause us to describe a child as gifted. Extraordinary capacity needs to be recognized and valued by both parents and children.

Opportunity must include early experiences which predispose a child to be intellectually active and interested, to solve her own problems, to make the most of her environment, to balance individual priorities and personal relationships, and to think of herself as confident and competent.

Personality may either facilitate or hamper the utilization of capacity and opportunity. Gifted children embody as many constellations of personality traits as are found in any large group of the population. Personality patterns become quite firmly fixed at a fairly early age. Mothers note these differences in infancy; however, the total pattern of response to the environment can be improved if a favorable family environment is consistently provided early in the child's life. Procrastination can be reduced but probably not erased. Shyness can be ameliorated but will probably always inhibit gregariousness. Aggressiveness can be channeled into productivity rather than confrontation. Big personality differences that can occur between children and parents need not damage the joyfulness of the relationship but they may necessitate a heightened awareness that although the child's interests and tendencies diverge widely from those of the parent, they are probably equally valid. Love is a relationship between one person and another which should contribute to the highest level of functioning for both. Many a child has had a profound influence on parents' personality and character development; the parent-child relationship exerts influence in both directions.

Anatole France wrote of parenting, "I would make lovable to her everything I wish her to love." I would ask, "What does she wish to love?" What do you wish your children to love and how do you strive to make those things lovable? What messages are you sending? Our political leaders and their public relations specialists place great emphasis on message-sending. Parents are children's major message senders. How are you listening to the messages your children are sending?

It must be admitted here that some tasks like homework

assignments may be low in stimulation and challenge to many of our gifted children. However, some humdrum activities usually must be done in order to avoid hassles and maintain responsibility. One of the questions parents frequently ask me is how they can get their child to complete homework assignments.

Actually, this question gives rise to many others that can not be addressed casually at a parent group meeting. In response to such questions, I suggest that parents explore several possible contributing factors.

First, is school work the major focus of parent-child interaction on a fairly regular basis, perhaps the only focus? Does the child obtain the undivided attention of either parent only around school issues? The child may be meeting his attention needs by procrastination around homework.

Second, has the homework policy been clarified with the youngster's teachers? When there are special programs or several teachers, unintentional overloading may sometimes occur. Does participation in a "pull-out" program complicate the issue?

Third, is the child prone to perfectionist tendencies which may seriously exacerbate the homework problem?

Each of the above would call for a different response from the parent and realization that, in the first and third instances, the homework problem is only a symptom of some deeper concern.

Having explored the above possibilities and finding no satisfactory explanation in any of those factors, we sometimes conclude that it is simply due to the natural human reluctance to perform unpleasant tasks. All of us have some things that have to be done that we just don't like to do, like cleaning the stove, balancing the checkbook, proofreading a report, mending or polishing something—boring but desirable. One strategy that has worked in some cases is for the parent to discuss this aspect of daily life with the child and plan to share the time that has to be devoted to homework by carrying out some parental task that is similarly distasteful but necessary. This provides excellent modeling, the reinforcement of sharing, it gets two boring jobs out of the way on a regular basis, and you can keep each other company in the process.

There is a great deal of similarity of good parenting advice for parenting all youngsters to that for parents of gifted youngsters. Setting limits, promoting responsible behavior, keeping communications open, modeling what you want your children to become.

Special notice should be given to the perceptivity and sense of fairness of gifted children and the futility of hypocrisy. Parents anguish over crucial advice about emerging sexuality and the conflict between overt social and moral precepts and their own personal experiences. Some good balance needs to be struck between every person's right to privacy, complete honesty in self-disclosure, and the recognition of the youngster's need for prudent guidance in this vital area of physical and emotional development. Perhaps the parent agonizing over the difference between what she is prescribing for her daughter and what she has carried out in her own earlier adolescence can think about how she might have managed her own sexuality if she had had the advantage of open and morally reasoned discussions of that aspect of her personhood with her parents. She might have decided on a different course of action—and she might not. In either case, can she look back on this activity, which she now wishes to conceal from her daughter because she doesn't want her daughter to imitate her own premarital sexual indulgence with her future spouse, and say that it has had a harmful effect on her eventual adulthood, marriage, and family?

We have discussed sex differences in many aspects of child-rearing, but little overt mention is made in popular literature of the common differences in what boys are told, by fathers, about emerging sexuality and what girls and boys are told by mothers about the same topic. The old double standard is alive and well, and it may be that many families wish to keep it that way. If that is so, such a value system should be made explicit to gifted youngsters or they will perceive differential advice as another example of meaningless, or pernicious, adult hypocrisy. If this is a problem area for parents, it will naturally be a problem area in child-rearing, and the healthiest course may be to admit to teenagers that incongruencies persist and to work together as a family in creative problem solving (Feldhusen and Treffinger 1977) or a rational decision making format (Applegate and Evans 1985) to come to shared decisions in such critical areas. Family counselors or parent group facilitators should be skilled in introducing families to such techniques. An article (Johnson and Roth 1985) has some concrete suggestions for productive strategies.

Since family value systems have priority in child-rearing philosophies, it would not be appropriate to advocate here specific solutions or answers to often-raised questions. What can be advocated are productive strategies for coping with problem situations and a commitment to becoming as well-informed as possible in any area of concern, which means digging out many sources and weighing each one's authority and relevance to a specific situation and individual.

Parents may increase their understanding of their role in stimulating and challenging a child by asking, "How do you think we have helped you the most?" and encouraging the child to draw a picture or write a story or poem in response. An alternative question might be, "Can you think of anything we have done to make you more interested in learning?" (Parker and Colangelo 1979).

The research of Freeman (1979) in England and Ward (1971) in the United States provides some unsettling matter for thought about the effect of social class on parent-child interaction in this area of stimulation and challenge.

In England, working-class mothers as compared to middle class mothers did not see the baby as a *developing human being* they could assist in growing. They felt relatively powerless and did not aid and encourage the child in the cognitively stimulating ways common to the British middle-class family.

In a poor black community in Louisiana, having much in common with poor black communities elsewhere in America, Ward found significant differences in mothers' perception of their babies and children from those commonly held by middle and upper class mothers. The little ones were not seen as individuals; mothers neither felt nor demonstrated any responsibility for providing for anything beyond food, clothing, and disciplinary needs of their children. The child was not seen as a *person* to talk with or to center one's attention on. The "good" child was either silent or outdoors.

Can such early environmental differences help to explain the over-representation of the middle and upper classes in identified populations of gifted children in our schools? The very behaviors that more sophisticated parents have learned to recognize as early signs of rich potential—insatiable curiosity, precocious language development, high energy level—are "bad" behaviors in many low socioeconomic status homes and would often be stifled by punishment and rejection.

The few hours daily spent after age three in Headstart settings may be too little and too late to bring about developmental change. What would probably be the most effective is television programming for adults in the format of the "soaps" that reach into millions of low socioeconomic status homes and could powerfully illustrate a different and possibly richer perspective on the nature of the child and the fascinating role of the mother and father in helping that child's mind as well as its body to grow. It doesn't take money; it does take awareness and time.

This is a challenge our more fortunate parents may want to respond to. Television writers and sponsors, arise!

11

Facilitating Creativity

C IVILIZATION depends on the exceptionally capable for innovation and progress. Although creative youngsters may offer the greatest hope for the improvement of the quality of human life and the future of life on our planet, such children are most likely to pass unrecognized through our educational assessment and identification nets. This is not always disastrous for either the individual or the larger society. Edison was taught at home by his mother. The family can more flexibly nurture and reinforce activities and interests which are difficult to accommodate in the group settings economically necessary for most schools.

The personality traits that contribute to creative productivity can be noted early and should be nurtured by parents in the home.

Freedom to explore and manipulate, time to daydream and fantasize, openness to the variety of ways of doing things are vital non-material gifts that parents can give to their offspring.

There is interesting research evidence of the ways in which varying child-rearing practices inhibit or foster creativity (Khatena 1978; Domino 1969; Grant and Domino 1976; Nichols 1964; Wallinga and Crase 1979).

The highly creative child is usually recognized early by parents and frequently characterized as "weird." The uninhibitable exploratory activity and seemingly limitless curiosity of these young children is often a nuisance for adults and an embarrassment to more socially conforming siblings. The more energetic and non-traditional a child's behavior is, the more likely that child will be curbed and squelched by parents and other family members.

As Paul Torrance, creator of creativity measures, tells us

(Khatena 1978, Foreword), research indicates that hereditary potential is not a powerful predictor of individual creative productivity. Rather, it is the influence of parents and significant others in home and school which determines to what extent the creative impulses will become sustained creative behaviors. Families can nurture creativity or stifle it even before a child reaches school age.

The challenge is for parents to perceive as fascinating and promising, even though trying, those "off-the-wall" behaviors and ideas. When parents, as well as teachers, can see these idiosyncratic activities only as troublesome, then their child-rearing practices will tend to suppress rather than foster creativity and the child may experience extreme difficulty in personal and social self-concept development.

The creatively gifted child is often a minority of one who must cope with the sanctions of social groups against that divergence. How can the child act on inspirations and inner drives without losing friends and alienating adults? Both parents and schools prize the "well-rounded" child, but some creatively gifted youngsters are powerfully drawn off-center and are truly eccentric in their involvement with their special talents and motivation. Many highly creative and talented adults who have made valuable contributions to knowledge and the arts have been singularly focused rather than well-rounded individuals. Perhaps parents and teachers overemphasize balance with highly creative children. Somehow, the burden for adjusting, "fitting-in," falls preponderantly on the gifted and creative child rather than being shared equally by the social groups of which the child is a member. It doesn't seem fair.

The creative child has perceptivity and values quite different from the group of which he is a member. Such a child needs parental understanding and help in order to safeguard the creativity without being obtrusive and unsocial. Parents cannot remove all of the obstructions in a child's life, but they can help the child to cope with them.

Of particular interest is the importance of the modeling by and interaction with the opposite-sex parent. Several researchers have noted the cross-sex parent's role in enhancing creativity (Lynn 1974; Wallinga and Crase 1979; Domino 1979) and indicate that fathers seem to be more influential in the creativity of daughters; mothers in the creativity of sons.

Fathers who take an active interest in doing things with gifted daughters, broadening their outlooks on the choices open to them and reinforcing their independent activities, are much more likely to find their female youngsters creatively productive than are fathers who reinforce daughters for stereotypically dependent or passive behaviors.

Mothers who pursue career or artistic interests of their own, often outside the home, seem to produce sons with more independence of thought and courage to be different than do mothers who are more attentive to and perhaps over-protective, smothering, of their little boys.

The best description of the findings of these many researchers exploring the family antecedents of creativity in gifted youngsters is embodied in the concept of androgyny, a breaking down of societal stereotypes of masculinity and femininity, permitting the expression in persons of either sex of the most effective human characteristics of both. This calls for truly creative parenting.

Traditionally, fathers have been described as "instrumental," the breadwinner, decision-maker, supplier of objective authority. In contrast, mothers have been perceived as "expressive," the nurturant caregiver providing emotional support, sometimes a buffer between father and child.

Those who have investigated the relationship between parent-child interaction and creativity in young boys and girls find that when fathers exhibit more of the expressive traits and mothers more of the instrumental behaviors, their opposite-sex children are more creative.

Warm, loving, accepting, and involved fathers and mothers who foster independence, curiosity, and flexibility appear to be modeling and encouraging the personality traits and motivational components which lead to creative productivity in their daughters and sons.

An interesting sidelight is that mothers who expressed high levels of concern for enhancing creativity and provided many materials in support of their children's creative activities did not have highly creative youngsters. It would appear that less imposed structure and less intense concern are desirable. One may recall the Lewis questionnaire in which parents assess the range of their support for a child's learning activities. If a parent can say yes to more than 30 of the 40 items, he or she may be focusing too intently or exclusively on the child and may need to give the youngster more room to maneuver.

As a young adult struggling with social adjustment problems in college classes, both with peers and professors, I was fortunately introduced by an experienced mentor to the notion of "creative conformity." This category of skills is part of what psychologists have called behavioral intelligence. It involves reading the priorities of other individuals and groups whose responses may affect your present and future well-being. It also involves a weighing of one's own priorities and identification of the most felicitous disposition of one's energies.

Then, in order to keep one's options open and preserve the opportunity to pursue valued personal goals, one can consciously decide to conform to group practices or institutional prescriptions in order to gain access to the credentials or connections which will open the necessary gates on one's chosen path.

This decision to inhibit self in some degree and conform in some school or social settings is not easy for the gifted child with his heightened sensitivity and well-developed conceptions of justice, but accommodation in inconsequential areas can leave him free to forge ahead in areas of larger significance. It can be a willed, not forced, choice to conserve energy for the things that really count.

If a youngster does quickly and satisfactorily those things which are important to teacher and parent, then both are much more likely to permit, even support, divergent activities which are important to the creative child.

Educators have often said that the most effective way for a classroom teacher to teach creativity is to be a creative person herself. The evidence for parental influence on creativity would indicate similar parameters. If parents wish to nurture creative potential and production in the child, they should make room in their lives for their own personal creativity. The fully competent parent is first a fully competent person whose openness to new ideas and joy in personal accomplishments provide strong and direct models for their youngsters.

In this respect, the personality profiles of creatively gifted individuals indicate a high level of individual androgyny. That is, creative boys show many of the traits which are stereotyped as "feminine", introspection, sensitivity, aesthetic values, etc. Creative girls, on the other hand, show many traditionally masculine traits, independence, assertiveness, ambition.

One can see in this the effect of opposite-sex parents whose interaction with son or daughter transcends traditional sex stereo-types and contributes to a strong self-image as an effective individ-ual rather than a "promising lad" or a "fine young woman."

One concomitant of the current reexamination of sex-roles in modern society may be emerging positive attitudes toward more androgynous individual development in which the ideal person can exhibit the finest characteristics of both the traditional stereo-types. The well-adjusted male can be nurturant, sensitive, and expressive as well as responsible, assertive, and daring. The well-adjusted female can be independent, highly competent, ambitious and instrumental as well as kind, helpful, and industrious. More innovation, more progress, might well ensue (Hollinger 1983). A need for more enlightenment in the schools is evident in the state-ment that teachers and other school personnel often associate giftedness with a variety of peculiarities, including social isolation, effeminacy in boys, aggressiveness in girls, and generally such high-strung behavior as nervousness or an overly sensitive tem-perament (Altman 1983).

A fanfare of attention is currently being given to the implica-tions of hemispheric organization of the brain for the nurturing of creative functions. I should not omit from this discussion of creativity some attention to the rising tide of right-brain pro-tagonists. One must be cautious in overinterpreting and overap-pyling the findings of medical and neurological research as some are presently doing—suggesting that learning disabilities can be cured by teaching to the right brain, or characterizing the left-hemisphere–dominated activities of classrooms as "half-brained." Still there are, beneath all the faddism, some important factors for which there is research evidence and which can profitably be considered when parents and teachers plan for well-balanced cur-ricular and extracurricular activities.

There is general agreement (Torrance 1980) that the left hemi-sphere of the brain seems to process information sequentially in a linear fashion, analytically and logically.

The right hemisphere processes information globally, rela-tionally, simultaneously, intuitively, in non-linear fashion.

In Western culture, the left cerebral cortex is the part of the brain we do our word things with, and it is very good with detail. Its primary role in school work activities is obvious.

Perceptual pattern-recognition, interrelatedness, the sense of beauty, are functions of the holistic right hemisphere and, for many people in our culture, are given inadequate opportunities for expression.

In an attempt to redress a perceived imbalance in learning experiences, some creativity crusaders would have us shut down the left-brain experiences to get fully in touch with right brain activities. But it must be remembered that the hemispheres are connected halves of one working entity, and that the integration, the interrelationship of the two hemispheres functioning together, defines our most productive efforts.

Operating solo, right brain experiences can be sublime, time-less, but tend to be inarticulate, vague, undefined, and produce little that is communicable to others. But the inspiration and intuition that this relatively untapped reservoir of perception can contribute to the specificity and linearity of the more familiar activities of the left hemisphere should engender a richly inte-grated productivity that draws on the best of both convergent and divergent thinking.

One of the giants in the study of giftedness and creativity is Carl Gowan whose intriguing perspectives are regularly published in the journals in our field. Recently, I listened to him in fascina-tion as he tellingly made the case for a more creative understand-ing of creativity. Although his emphasis was on the transcendent quality of inspirational experiences, intense and inexpressible, he noted that the translation of that inspiration into artistic or scien-tific breakthroughs is dependent on the skills and knowledge that have been built up in what could well be described as "left-brain" experiences. He likens the subconscious (right hemisphere?) of the creative person to a stereo receiver and the conscious, pragmatic (left-hemisphere?) to the tuner. He did not insert these references to hemisphericity, but I drew analogies as I listened and heard in his unique presentation valuable support for integration of learn-ing experiences. Logical, sequential, linear thinking (Guilford's convergent thinking) should not be devalued in the hot pursuit of holistic, intuitive, relational thinking (Guilford's divergent think-ing). At home and at school, children should be encouraged to function in both modalities and to find satisfaction in the integra-tion of both dimensions of brain activity. Thomas Edison is re-ported to have stated that "invention is 99 percent perspiration and 1 percent inspiration." The most productively creative people work very hard at learning as much as possible about the pragmatics of their art so that when those rare time-out-of-mind transcendent flashes of inspiration come they can be effectively transmitted into the temporal patterns of innovative problem-solving in a chosen field. For Mozart into music, for Eliot into poetry, for Kekuli into the benzene ring and for all of us, into a richer life.

The need of the thinker to cast embryonic ideas into language in order to understand them better himself was best described by the noted author Saul Bellow. He asked, "How does a person know what he thinks until he sees what he has to say about it—either orally or in writing?" Language production helps most humans to organize thought. Nonverbal forms of expression—pictorial, musical, kinetic—help to express thought and feeling more directly and are more personal and individual. Their meaning is often communicated at a less rational, although intensely valued level.

Earlier in this chapter it was recommended that parents help the highly individualistic creative child to maintain positive relationships within a group. Pauline Pepinsky (1960) described some very useful strategies which parents can teach to youngsters in jeopardy of experiencing adjustment difficulties.

1. Translate your ideas into language accessible and relevant to others so that they can see your contribution as instrumental to their own needs (or at least not in conflict with them).

2. State any criticism of others in a positive and helpful way.

3. Make it evident that basically you stand for something that commands the respect of others in the group—values, principles, ideals.

4. Minimimze your personal threat to others by granting them dignity; listen patiently.

5. Build up a "credit rating" and purchase more individual freedom over a period of time by initial cooperation with prevailing demands and requirements, wherever these do not seriously conflict with your personal integrity.

6. Focus on the job to be done, not on "personalities," or on acquiring status as an end in itself.

7. Take into account matters of timing so that you are able to delay response as well as to act.

These strategies will assist the creatively gifted individual, child or adult, to resolve the conflict between maintaining independence and conforming to the needs of the group. This Creative

Conformity will permit productive nonconformity and preserve personal equilibrium.

I have seen in my own counseling work examples of the sort described by other authorities on creatively gifted children (Gowan 1955; Torrance 1962; Khatena 1978). Prolonged enforced repression of the intellectual and expressive needs of the creative child may lead to emotional problems and neurosis, even psychosis.' Neuroses can be induced by intense and continued anxiety states which occur when the youngster cannot understand the rejection and frustration of natural tendencies and activity drives (Dirkes 1983). When creative energies are seriously blocked, the child's thinking can become paralyzed. Escape into imagination can blur distinctions between reality and fantasy. Such a child may develop defending behaviors similar to those of psychotics. Such extreme maladjustment is uncommon, but some degrees of stress are experienced by all nonconforming children.

It is not necessary to suffer in order to be creative, but it seems that if one is creative there follows suffering. The psychologically secure base of the family can deflect the resentments of the militant conformists and strengthen the self-understanding and self-acceptance of the child who dances to a melody unheard by others. For the young renegade baffled by the failure of peers, teachers, even family, to understand, I recommend the slim book, *A Different Kind of Boy* (Hise 1979).

Some years ago, John Gowan (Gowan and Torrance 1971) made some helpful suggestions for parents who cherish their children's mental health and happiness. These guidelines incorporate and summarize much of this chapter and might form a useful self-examination for parents. They describe truly empowering parental roles, fostering a rich and productive self-reliance. I have paraphrased them in light of some of Gowan's more recent work and have added some parenthetical comments from my own current work.

1. Provide a warm safe psychological base from which to explore, and to which the child may return when he is frightened by his own discoveries.

2. Be supportive of the child's ability to create and sympathetic to early failure. Avoid setting up unfavorable evaluation of the child's attempts to create. (It is not helpful to tell the child how the product could be improved, "This is nice but it could be so much better if . . ." so that no matter how hard a

child tries, the outcome is not quite good enough. Some parents mistakenly respond in this way out of their high opinion of the child's ability and well-meant desire to spur the child to ever-greater achievement. The actual outcome is a gifted adult who is never quite sure of her own adequacy, unable to feel fully a sense of comfortable accomplishment—the spur becomes a goad that never disappears.)

3. Be genuinely tolerant of new or strange ideas, respectful of a child's curiosity and questioning and ideas. Seek to answer all his questions even though they may seem wild or "far out."

4. Let the child be alone and carry out things on her own if she wishes, for too much supervision can hinder this productivity. (Their whims and goals are their own, and the well-meant help or assistance of a parent may be resisted as intrusive and distracting, a violation of personal privacy of mind. Even very young gifted children show sturdy resistance to parents who seek too strenuously to enjoy vicariously the innermost workings of the creative imagination.)

5. Help the child learn how to build his personal value system, not necessarily relying totally on his own views, so that he will know how to value both himself, his ideas, and other persons and their ideas. He can, thus, in turn, be appropriately valued by others.

6. Help her to satisfy basic human needs (bodily safety, love, esteem of self and others), for a person whose energies are bound up in basic needs is less able to explore the heights of self-fulfillment.

7. Help him to handle disappointments and doubts when he stands alone in some creative act which peers do not understand so that he will maintain his creativity, finding reward within himself and worrying less about the approval of others. That may be slow in coming, but it will eventually come. (In this connection, personal journals and autobiographies of other creative men and women can help the child to realize that he is not alone in his struggles. Official biographies by admiring disciples often minimize eccentricity or the estrangement experienced by creative giants.)

8. Help her to understand that there are areas of her life where there is more than one answer to a question, and other areas where there are as yet no answers because the question is not well asked. She can learn to live with intellectual tension without aborting the ideas that produce it.

9. Help the child to value himself as a creative person even though you have to show disapproval for some of his

behavior that is not socially acceptable. (An incisive verbal caricature of an acquaintance can be very perceptive and witty, but very unkind.)

10. Help her to lean far into herself to capture floating (preconscious) ideas. Give sympathy rather than disapproval to her early and crude attempts to describe these ideas and make them socially acceptable. (There is some evidence that such transcendent preconscious fantasies are the inchoate raw source of true creative inspiration.)

11. Praise his new-born creative efforts, avoid criticizing initial creative outcomes, no matter how crude. Do this in an air of warm and affectionate expectancy for a child tends to create not only for himself but also for those he loves.

12. Help her to be a "reasonable adventurer" and take reasonable cognitive risks and inituitive leaps, for by so doing, she is most likely to hit upon a real discovery or breakthrough.

13. Maintain the essential climate for creativity while helping him to avoid public disapproval, reduce social tensions, and cope with peer sanctions. Thus, he can become a constructive rather than nonconstructive nonconformist. The more we open channels for productive activities, the more we tend to close off the vents of destructive behaviors. A child who is denied good creative outlets may become creatively devious in undesirable ways.

14. Go to some lengths to locate at least one other playmate of similar age and ability. It is very important for a school age child to have a same-sex peer that she can get along with and who likes her. A gifted girl, one in a hundred, has to know about 100 other children to find one like herself and if that hundredth child is a boy, she has a problem, for same-sex playgroupings are the powerful social norm of the schoolyard and neighborhood playground. She needs another girl who may be 8 but thinks like 11. It may take some parental searching and chauffeuring, but it is preferable to letting her develop lonely antisocial habits because no one else seems to like her.

Be aware that when an elementary school child becomes so absorbed in her own activities that she does not have friends, it is because she has not had a chance to make the right kind (Gowan and Torrance 1971).

The sensitive balance between supporting and freeing embodied in these paragraphs will help parents to cherish the child who is different.

Parents can and should explore some of the newly devised

strategies for creative problem solving and practice those strategies in resolving family problems. This is one of the best ways to model for the creative child the search for alternative strategies when the initially tried approach meets with too much resistance. Excellent sources are DeBono (1970, 1971); Feldhusen and Treffinger (1977); Elberle and Stanish (1980); Khatena (1982).

Get your parent group involved—it's fun!

12

Supporting Special Interests
and Talents

Most important, perhaps, is to have confidence in your child's capacity to grow. He will tend to take what he needs from the favorable environment you provide. This confidence in the child's inner resources is a prerequisite to respect for him. The adult is a facilitator, not a pusher or puller" (Strang 1960).

What is a *favorable* environment which will most wholesomely nurture special interests and talents of the individual child? One of the first things that parents ask is what they should be doing to provide appropriate opportunities and resources to ensure their child's fullest development. This question is asked most frequently, and with highest anxiety, in situations where a child has just been screened by the school staff and identified as "gifted." For some parents this is not a surprise, but for many the news engenders an immediate concern—"Are we doing the right things?"

My first response to such worried queries is that this is the same child as she was before the label was attached and it is unlikely that any drastic changes should ensue. In fact, the recognition by the schools that she has special capabilities can be seen as evidence that parents are doing many things right. But, sometimes, with the best of intentions, parents can overdo. For example, one ten-year-old boy from an upper-middle-class family, when asked in an interview if there was one thing he might change if he could, responded that he would really like to have the whole family at home together more often. The school-age children were so over-

111

scheduled in after-school enrichment opportunities and the parents very active in worthwhile special interest areas, that it seemed to this lad that they were never all together at home as a family.

Family experience may be the most enriching of all and must, if need be, be purposefully included in the scheduling.

With that caveat, it is fair to say that some special provisions probably do need to be made in order to broaden the gifted child's horizon of choices and to provide for the higher level of performance of which the gifted child is capable. As was indicated earlier, parents of exceptionally able children do have to take significant responsibility for their children's educational enrichment beyond what most schools are equipped or funded to offer. In the best of situations, this will be a cooperative arrangement with the school, but it must be admitted that this is often not the case. In a later chapter, we will explore some possibilities for improving parent-school-child relationships.

In carrying out their parental responsibilities for providing challenge in the child's environment, something very human often happens. It is quite difficult for a person who has received great satisfaction and enjoyment from a particular kind of excelling in a chosen field to refrain from vigorously steering the child into the same line of achievement. "If this has been so great for me, how can wrestling not be great for my son, even if he doesn't see it now—it is obvious that he can do it well. Later on, he will enjoy being so good at this, besides, he does like it, look how often he practices!" Those words of a caring, intelligent, athletically excelling father have to be contrasted with the soft-spoken comments of his mother in a separate interview, "Yes, he practices hard and participates in all the meets because he knows how much it means to his father and he likes making his dad proud." What the youngster genuinely showed most interest in was science experiments, for which he received much less reinforcement from his father. With a gifted youngster, both talents can usually be accommodated but what is missing in the described family is true respect for the child and his own interests.

This brings us to the second important word from the quote, *respect*. One of the terms given tremendous play in educational circles is "respect for individual differences." This is a value that ought to be held and acted on just as strongly in the family circle.

In earlier chapters, there is a discussion of helping children to understand differences in abilities as the family finds the most positive responses to a variety of gifts. In addition to the differences in abilities, there are also differences in interests. Respect for this dimension of the individuality of the gifted child may be a less perceived area of need in parent-child relationships.

Gifted youngsters who have multipotentiality for career development, who can do many things well often have a difficult time choosing a career path, since making one choice may well close off others of competing interest. The choice should, however, be the youngster's. Parents should avoid stepping in too strongly in directing the decision. In the study of careers of gifted individuals, we find that they often have as many as three successive careers in adulthood. It is possible that, on his own, a youngster will come around to the field that had first priority for the parent—but it will have been his choice. For most fields, deferred decision is not a problem, but in some areas, to reach the top means an early start and a very narrow focus.

If a highly talented child shows early signs on her own of a desire for intensive involvement in a special field like music, mathematics, dance, or athletics and freely devotes a major portion of leisure time to that single pursuit, then she may have both the singular talent and consuming enjoyment of a narrow area of activity that is characteristic of a very few who reach eminence in a chosen field. They may even strenuously resist efforts aimed at well-roundedness or balance.

For a group of outstanding performers in several fields, Bloom (Bloom and Sosniak 1981) has described the pattern of child-rearing and educational practices which brought a special talent to full flower. He tells us that the most striking finding in the research he and his colleagues have done through interviews with eminent musicians, mathematicians, Olympic swimmers, is the very active role of the family in the support and encouragement of these individuals. He indicates that not one of them could have reached that top level of achievement on his or her own! "While it may be debatable as to whether any of these individuals is a genius, the old saw that 'genius will out' in spite of circumstances is not supported by this study of talent development. Whatever the individuals' original 'gifts' or early abilities, skills, and achievements, without extremely favorable supporting and teaching circumstances over more than a decade they would not have been likely to reach the levels of attainment for which they were selected in this study" (Bloom 1982, p. 511).

In all of these individuals parents believed very early that the child had exceptional aptitude in a specific area. These qualities made a great difference in their expectations for the child. They embarked on a course of action which has many implications for the family and the child which other parents will want to consider as they respond to the challenge of cherishing the child who is gifted.

In the majority of the cases Bloom studied, one or both parents, or a close relative, had a prior personal interest in the talent area and greatly encouraged the child in that specific field. Often this is done in the hope that the child will reach the heights to which the parent aspired but was unable to attain. This is especially true of mothers whose individual goals have been subordinated (often willingly) to the needs of home and family. I referred in the opening chapters to the desire in some parents to shine vicariously through their gifted children. Such self-aggrandizement through the child is seldom acknowledged even in self-awareness, but it sometimes lies at the heart of the overwhelming family focus on the nurturance and stellar achievement of the most promising child (Feldman, R.D., 1982).

It would be difficult to analyze the early motivation and determine whether it was child-initiated or parent-initiated. Whichever may have been the case, all of these prodigies received early and constant encouragement from parents. In some of the families, parental commitment in a chosen area, music, sports, etc., was so intense that all members of the family were expected to participate. A child would find it almost impossible to resist such pressure, and of course the pressure would be even greater upon the most talented. This parental influence is a major factor in the years from three to seven. In most of the homes studied, it was assumed that, just as the child naturally wants to learn to talk, he or she just as naturally wishes to acquire the talent to which the parent is devoted. The children are almost never consulted or presented with alternate choices.

In the first stages of development, the talented parent is the tutor, model, and reinforcer and the child is still playing with the talent. In the second stage, when the child begins school, a special teacher is employed for one-to-one instruction in the area of talent and that training is more important than the group instruction which takes place in the school classroom. The design of the instruction is also different. For the tutor or coach, each child was seen as unique and the pace, level, and reward for the tasks were controlled by the child's carefully monitored growth.

There was continual adjustment to the child learning the talent, which contrasts with the child having to continually adjust to the pace and level of the group in most school settings. When a child was progressing poorly in the hands of a tutor or coach, parents assumed that the tutor was at fault and sought another teacher. This does have parallels in parent-school interactions.

Although the selected teacher is central to the second stage of talent development, the home still plays an important role in carrying out the teacher's directions and supervising practice. Tutors often re-order the entire family's schedule to accommodate the lessons and practice of the budding prodigy (one star skater's sister's responsibility was making her costumes). There was a high level of consistency between the teacher's methods and the parental reinforcement and reward. In the second stage, the child began to evidence willingness to work and achieve a high standard.

In the third stage, as the youngster's ability begins to outstrip that of the parents, more highly skilled teachers are sought and the talent development becomes less of a partnership between parents and teacher. The master teacher becomes the sole arbiter of the instructional process and the role of the parents becomes one of emotional and material support. I know all readers are aware of special cases in which families relocate in order to find a special teacher; or parents live separately for a considerable time so that a mother can accompany a young child to a distant training program; a child of 11 or 12 may be sent to live with a foster family in another city or country in order to receive specialized instruction. American tennis schools are a notorious example.

In this third stage, public events, recitals, contests, awards, become an important component of the development of special talent, and events taking place outside the home acquire precedence. These activities tend to place parents in the audience.

In the first stage, the child is emulating the parent. In the second stage, there is partnership between parent and the teachers they select. In the third stage, the parents are subordinate to the master teacher who often selects the pupils and who is the chief model for those pupils.

In the fourth stage, the truly outstanding individual outdistances even the best of teachers and emulates only the few others who have stood out in the chosen field.

Very, very few ever reach the rarefied heights, and we all feel enriched in experiencing their performance. But parents ought to consider carefully both the advantages and disadvantages to the child and to the family. What is to be said about the many other children who are brought into the above process and are winnowed out along the way?

In order to embark on the path Bloom described, a parent would want to be sure of the child's own motivation and supported by experts in the identification of the child's unique potential. The cues which parents and tutors perceived in the early identification of actual prodigies may be of interest to other parents who are discovering dimensions of giftedness in their own children (Bloom 1982).

Those who became outstanding musicians showed very early a great sensitivity and emotional responsivity to music. They usually had perfect pitch and were able to "play by ear" complicated tunes and harmonies as preschoolers.

The talented mathematicians showed, prior to age eight, learning characteristics that are more common to adolescents. They did much purposeful question asking of adults and made effective use of the answers, quite different from the age-typical endless why's. They played alone happily for hours and often became lost in solitary thinking, even when playmates were available. They pursued a great deal of independent learning from books or observation of others. A large number experienced relative difficulty in reading and were not recognized by the school as especially gifted until high school

The Olympic swimmers were described at quite an early age (three to four) as very much at ease in water and having a very special feel for effective and graceful movement in the water.

All were characterized early by rapid learning of new skills, and later showed high levels of willingness to work, competitiveness, and determination to do one's personal best. They became single-minded in the pursuit of excellence and by adolescence were spending more time on the talent area than any other aspect of life or learning. And so were many of the families. In fact, Bloom indicates that the commitment and support of parents is a primary determinant of great talent development.

It can be seen readily that the parental attitudes described in

Bloom's work are poles apart from those of parents who want their child to just be normal and who choose to down play their unique gifts.

There should be a moderate middle ground which would encourage without hot-housing, and recognize without misplaced egalitarianism the special talents and interests of gifted children.

In providing a favorable environment, parents would be sensitive to the interests of the child and encourage exploration by children of either sex of all the possibilities for intellectual and creative growth. Here, too, prudence should be exercised. Avoid the pitfall of rushing pell-mell into the purchase of expensive equipment or contracting for extensive training until the youngster has had sufficient exposure to a new field to be assured of a genuine and sustained involvement. Gifted children are intrigued by almost everything, but initial fascinations may fade early upon a fuller acquaintance with a new attraction. If parents feel obligated to do everything possible to provide every opportunity for the child to express his potential then they may make considerable investments of time and money in response to the child's first indication of interest. Then they are very frustrated and disappointed when that first glow of enthusiasm fades and the expensive equipment is neglected. Parents may even become angry and nag and punish the child. It would be better to go easy in the beginning and hold firm against the child's pleas for every available component of top-of-the-line accoutrements. Gifted children experience a new interest intensely; they are talented at identifying all of the best gear; and they are highly articulate and persuasive.

Do not feel that you are failing to fulfill adequately your parental responsibility in challenging and enriching your gifted child when you are being prudent in refusing to plunge headlong into expenditures in a new area before the child has really tested out her commitment to it. You will save yourself and the child from recrimination and guilt over wasted resources if you go slowly. Prudence is one virtue in which parents usually excel their gifted progeny and strategies of foresight are much more effective than hindsight in reducing tension and nagging between parent and child.

Another *favorable* condition is the willingness of a parent to explore a new interest with the child. This is the converse of the situation where the parent pulls the child into the parent's area of special interest.

The parent need not be an expert in the child's chosen area of exploration, but a genuine openness to new learning is essential, along with skills in question-asking and problem-identification. There should be no reluctance on the part of either father or mother to admit neophyte status in a particular field in which they have no experience; parents don't have to be all-knowing, just all-loving. You may be surprised at the relationships to be discovered between your acquired areas of expertise and the new ideas your child wishes to explore. Your own enthusiasm for life-long learning and willingness to search in new directions are the best models for intellectual growth that your child can have.

The *respect* a parent accords the individual interests of each child permits the child to give priority to activities other than those the parents find the most attractive or enjoyable to themselves. Give the child the time and space to taste a little or a lot of all the many things that seem worth investigating and be both flexible and prudent in the indulgence of those interests.

Comment must be made here on the tendency of parents to overschedule gifted children in many activities. This often happens because the child is multi-talented and has shown broad interests. Sometimes parents indicate that that want to make certain that no latent ability or possible flair may be overlooked in the nurturing of the child's full potential.

For a four-year-old girl, it seems that daily nursery school, Saturday morning lessons at the art museum, story hour at the library, and gymnastics lesson are overdoing it! Such a weekly schedule leaves little time for simply being. The juggling of transportation schedules for her working parents who also have a younger child also means less family time together.

Perhaps it would be interesting to ask this gifted four-year-old to list her optional outside activities in order of her own preferences (Mom insists that she enjoys them all) and cut the schedule in half, respecting her priorities and giving her more free time for private thought and self-originated activities. She enjoys these, too.

If at all possible, each child in a family should have some space of his or her own, inviolable, to work on projects, store collections, keep special possessions and maintain some personal clutter. This often offends the need for tidiness and order that many mothers feel duty bound to preserve. When limits to each person's special space are set, it is easier to keep each individual's prized clutter within designated bounds. For very young children this practice also lays the groundwork for understanding the rights of the individual and the private personhood of both mother and father. It is an early concrete experience of respect for the individual, both awarded to and expected from the child.

When any one child in a family is found to have a special ability, it is quite likely that brothers and sisters have superior abilities also. The unique strengths of each child may vary a great deal, and parenting skills are stretched in the effort to bring harmony rather than competition, frustration, or jealousy to the family circle. Creative children need creative parents who can devise cooperative projects in which each sibling can contribute a unique talent and receive gladly the complementary contribution of a sibling with a quite different talent. We have already mentioned the jointly produced book in which writing talents, editing talents, illustrating talents, problem-solving skills, production abilities, entrepreneurial talents, shared activities or hobbies, can all be combined in *Sibling Synergy* to generate a highly successful product. The whole is greater than the sum of its parts.

Surely this is preferable to a star-oriented family constellation in which the first priority for parents and sisters and brothers is the care and feeding of the one prodigy for whom the family becomes a retinue.

Should a highly gifted boy be radically accelerated and sent on to college at age 14 or 15? There are many subquestions to that larger one. Will he have to live away from home? What are the ages of his current friends? What can the area schools offer as acceptable alternatives to early admission to college when it means separation from the family? Would summer experiences with similarly gifted age peers be a more attractive option? Why is the family considering early college? Did the idea originate with the youngster, the school counselor, the parent? Has anyone he knows done this? Has the family which is considering such a move sought out as much information, both pro and con, which they can obtain?

If such questions are explored before an action is taken, the questions about responding to the unhappiness of a poorly adjusted precocious college student would become less frequent. Because personal identity and ego integration are the primary psychosocial tasks of the age in question (Erikson 1963), it is not surprising that some early entrance students do not adjust at all well. It must be said here that some of these early placements work out very well, especially if the young person can continue to live at home and work through the social and emotional developmental priorities in the supportive environment of understanding parents and siblings.

If the early college entrance entails separation from home and friends, then much more serious thought must be given to the search for desirable alternatives which will promote continued optimal growth in areas of talent while not prematurely cutting off the psychosocial security of the home base. As stated earlier, opportunities for learning are available from many sources in addition to the traditional schools and from many people outside the family, but only the family can provide the nurturant, supportive environment which is vital for healthy personality growth. The learning opportunities will probably still be out there in several years but the time of critical development will not be postponed. Of course, every case is individual and the emotional and social life of a unique youngster may be unsatisfactory in a current educational setting—to such an extent that desperate and radical changes appear preferable. Let me just gently say that, usually, when the youngster himself is consulted, the preference is almost always to remain with near age peers. We simply cannot overestimate the importance of friendship in the young person's self-concept, as well as the positive regard of significant others, including teachers as well as parents.

It should be noted that there are some outstanding exceptions which are presently occuring in at least two fairly well-established programs. In discussion with staff members of Midwest Talent Search and Julian Stanley's program, it emerges that when a summer experience on a college campus with similar age peers has taken place, some highly gifted young people initiate the request for early full admission to college. On campuses where there is an already known age cohort and a recognized program of support and counseling for these youngsters, positive experiences are taking place. On one campus, the major problem encountered was inability to obtain a driver's license due to the student's tender years. One simply cannot generalize about the advisability of early admission. Each case is individual. All of the factors described must be explored both with the student and the college.

Many times it is the affective, or socioemotional climate of the educational setting which has most impact on the child—and the frustrated parents may settle on an academic solution because it is easier to implement. This is admittedly an extremely complex problem and one which must be considered in all its individual ramifications in each case. If the student is a girl, the family may want to consider other factors. Again, I recommend some family participation in creative problem solving or rational decision making strategies.

Cherish the child, in all her aspects and facets and settings, of which the special gift is only a lovely part.

PART IV

Sharing

13

Working Productively with the Schools

C OOPERATION rather than confrontation should be the thrust of parental interaction with the schools. Parents should begin with the assumption that teachers do want all of the children in their classrooms to learn and prosper to the best of their abilities. No teacher wishes to teach inadequately or cause negative feelings in pupils. Most teachers do the best they are capable of and work very hard for very slim rewards. But few, too few, teachers have any training for working with gifted and talented youngsters, and relatively few are intellectually gifted themselves.

In addition to the lack of appropriate training for the majority of classroom teachers, many school administrators, products of the egalitarian American society, share the widespread resistance to a so-called elitism in programing for gifted learners.

We need to understand the training and values of these genuinely dedicated school people and, within that framework of good intentions, strive to come to fruitful answers to some pressing questions.

How can parents help individual teachers to meet their children's educational and social needs?

Can parents honestly accept the teacher's perception of their child?

How can parents bring about change in administrator attitudes that stand in the way of appropriate educational environments?

Let us examine at some length the first question. Most parents have some awareness of the child's superior mental functioning even prior to school entry and many have children tested for early admission because of their child's precocious abilities.

For some families, the adversary relationship begins almost immediately as they are forced to exert much pressure upon school authorities who generally oppose early admission, usually on grounds of social immaturity. From my own experience, both as parent and educator, I would not make a blanket endorsement for early admission of any child who qualifies by IQ testing alone (usually two standard deviations above the mean, or about 130 IQ). There are many facets other than scores on highly vocabulary-loaded tests that affect an individual child's need for early school entry.

When parents ask for my advice or support in these cases, I always insist on some extended interaction with the child, and with the parents. Why do the parents wish the child to enter school early? Some reply that "well, she can easily do the work," or "he's way ahead in his nursery school and we think he should go on." In a limited number of cases, especially for highly gifted children whose friends are already older than they are, I have agreed with the parents' position and recommended early admission.

However, the question must always be asked whether the flexibility and freedom to explore of the preschool child's world should be so readily sacrificed to the group-oriented regimentation of the institutionalized school. Investigation of the world and direct experiences are the rich opportunities available in home and neighborhood, in libraries, museums, and parks. Space and time for fantasy and imagination outside the boundaries of class periods and assignments offer desirable dimensions which will enhance future development of the child's potential to a much greater extent than most early school experiences in traditional settings. I would like also at this point to revisit earlier discussion of the central role of the home and family in the nurturing of a stable and positive self-concept in the gifted child. Early admission to formal schooling can result in a truncation of that process by shortening the years of close and extended parental contact. Gifted youngsters often grow up and away from parents at an earlier age than their less able peers, and it seems a shame to hasten that time even more by early separation of the child from the home setting. I cannot overstate the primacy of the family in the emotional, personal health of the child. Educational opportunities will be available throughout the youngster's life and may be more advantageously encountered from a strong base of emotional security and experiential variety gained in the preschool years. If parents look at school as only a part, as formidable a part as it is, of the child's education they may consider more factors when thinking about early admission.

Having written this, I must indicate that all cases are individual and, for some children early admission is a positive step.

Some talents, like mathematical genius, emerge early, and rapid completion of formal schooling, even through the graduate level, permits mathematical and some scientific prodigies freedom for the creative work which takes place most productively in young adulthood. Access to the resources of good educational settings facilitates their natural, albeit unique, intellectual development.

Musical talents similarly emerge very early, but such gifts are customarily nurtured outside of traditional school settings and early training is rather easily obtained. Music schools are much more receptive to prodigies than regular schools and have never been asked to be concerned over social development.

Other gifts, especially in the areas of the humanities, literature, philosophy, mature more slowly and would be less benefited by abbreviation of the preschool years.

Considerations of physical size at age four or five are of less concern. There is so much natural variability in size, even with age peers, and I have seen quite tiny youngsters make good kindergarten and first grade adjustments because of their self-confidence and social skills.

If, after careful weighing of all these factors and consultation with experienced experts, parents decide to seek early admission for the child, they should listen respectfully to the professional educators' concerns about such exceptions. Not all cases work out well, and those are the ones that stick in the administrator's mind because they caused problems and may have reinforced an already negative view of the practice.

Parents should respond with a discussion of their careful consideration of many points and a polite but firm description of their reasons for requesting appropriate special treatment. Other very young children with unique attributes are accorded appropriate educational consideration; hearing impaired children receive early schooling in order to facilitate language development. No one quarrels with that.

Potential for achievement can be demonstrated by test scores and interviews. Actual performance can be evaluated by observation in the classroom setting, with a receptive teacher. Be willing to discontinue the experience if all does not go well. The child's enjoyment of life rather than parental disappointment is the first priority.

If early admission is not approved by school administration, suitable alternatives can still be sought. Do not waste energy and emotional resources in bitterness or resentment. Parent-school enmities have a way of bringing adversity down on the heads of the children who get caught in the middle. Seek instead a desirable preschool setting with a philosophy and a program that are positive for gifted children. Features to look for, in addition to positive teacher attitude are:

> 1. *Flexibility*—the gifted child's predilection for staying with an engrossing task beyond some scheduled time period calls for tolerance rather than the frustration of enforced activity shifts.
> 2. *Emphasis on social development*—because of intellectual precocity, many young gifted children show a strong tendency to isolation from age peers in their chosen activities. They need contrast, early encouragement to engage in group activities and to experience sharing, cooperation, successes, and failures with other children. They need to learn friend-making and friend-keeping skills which will stand them in good stead in the (for-them) socially trying climate of the regular schools.
> 3. *Deemphasis of academic activities*—the ability to perform school tasks is not necessarily an indicator of the appropriateness of the early introduction of such structure into the life of a four-year-old.

I have already written of the value of the freedom of those exploratory years in building the strongest possible base for later, more-structured, learning activities. Parental egos and parental comparisons can bring about insidious pressures on preschoolers (and their teachers) to read. It seems that the age of reading-onset is a badge of the level of giftedness in many parental discussions. I can recall so many highly gifted little ones who simply were more interested in numbers or bugs than letters and shrugged off all efforts to induce them to read early. In other lamentable instances, over-solicitous parents have produced children who refused to read as a passive-resistance tool in manipulating parental attention and concern. A little more parental nonchalance about reading seems a most welcome response. The direct experiences of the child's world will contribute much more to eventual reading acuity and enjoyment than overemphasized early literacy. If the child wants to read, fine! If not, relax and feel secure in the confidence that reading will come with relative ease when the interest is there. Reading experts tell us that what children bring to the printed page is just as important as the marks on that page. Even learning disabled gifted youngsters learn to read successfully although with less speed and some compensatory strategies. However, in the majority of cases, the absence of reading precocity is the result of disinterest rather than disability and should not become a matter of concern or ego-involvement for parents.

Whether at early or conventional admission age, school entry can be a very difficult adjustment time for the gifted child. Parents, teachers, and enlightened administrators need to work together to make it a positive experience for all.

The groundwork in self-concept and understanding of giftedness which has been laid down at home provides the basis for good responses from the child. Parental training should help the child to avoid arrogance with age peers and needless clashes with not-always-expert adults. Parents can also help by reinforcing the concept of creative conformity and the selective inhibiting of resistance-arousing behaviors in the interest of rewarding social relationships with peers and less friction with teacher. Direct parental contribution to the classroom setting will be discussed in the following chapter.

Teachers in kindergarten and first grade usually give special priority to assisting all their pupils in making the transition from home to school, and we know that lengthy parent-teacher conferences are common in those entry years. However, most teachers have not been exposed to any in-depth preparation for working with gifted pupils. If any training in differentiating instruction has been given, it has frequently been in the area of "mainstreaming" the handicapped learners. Of course, gifted learners have always been mainstreamed but seldom with any mandated attention to their special needs. So, even with the best of intentions, many teachers intensify rather than reduce the adjustment problem. Listed below are a few pitfalls which should be avoided, and perhaps diplomatic parents in pre-entry interview with teachers can assist them in avoiding some well-meant but potentially harmful practices.

1. Teachers should not over-emphasize competitive learning games which the most gifted child will almost invariably win, causing early resentment among peers and not bringing about the general motivation the teacher intended.

2. Teachers should avoid reinforcing the gifted child's perfectionist tendencies by over-praising the best or the neatest product. They should not single out the gifted child for outstanding academic performance but rather encourage co-operative activities and enthusiastic participation processes.

3. Teachers should avoid show-casing a highly gifted child or making of her a prodigy in the eyes of peers, other teachers, and administrators. Natural excellence will be truly recognized and the misplaced parading by others of a pupil's extraordinary achievements usually brings about resentment, jealousy, and often rejection, rather than the anticipated approbation. The other extreme of intentional public down-playing of unique abilities and even sarcastic teacher responses to superior performances is of course unacceptable and should result in a room change.

4. Teachers should be accepting of intuitive and atypical learning strategies. Most gifted children neither need nor can respond to the high structure and repetitive reinforcement activities which are desirable for many primary grade pupils of average ability. Teachers often need the assistance of a special resource teacher to help them differentiate curriculum to meet the unique needs of the highly gifted. Parents should be strongly supportive in this area.

I must also make a balancing recommendation here for parents in parent-teacher interviews. As difficult as it may be, parents should attend very carefully to the teacher's perceptions of their child. I have often seen pupils whose classroom behavior bears little relationship to home behavior and sometimes the negative classroom behaviors are symptomatic of family situations that may need reexamination. The teacher is usually giving parents an accurate description of behavior he or she has observed. The teacher's interpretation of the causes of such behavior may be less accurate—or they may be right on target, and the teacher is trying to be helpful. It is possible that excessive parental pressures for achievement or a desire for more attention at home may be a factor in school problems (even though many teachers do not have an adequate understanding of giftedness). Try not to reject teacher comments too hastily without exploring family interactions as an area that might need some adjustments.

Experience has convinced me that the most beneficial attribute of the school administrator is a genuinely positive attitude toward responding effectively to the individual differences among pupils. This will support flexibility in curriculum and scheduling and allow teachers innovative modifications to traditional practices. Administrators should be receptive rather than resentful of parental concerns and take some personal responsibility for reducing the adversary relationships that too frequently develop.

Often parents wait until misunderstandings mount and dissatisfaction accumulates and then storm the school on a tide of frustration and hostility. Do not let such situations build. A parent should, without being a nit-picking nuisance, try to resolve small problems as soon as they arise, and, through a friendly but firm approach to the school, make clear their concern for an appropriate educational setting for children of superior ability. Make the school aware of your willingness to share responsibility in the education of your child. Educate yourself on research and best practices in gifted education and be forthcoming with support for good efforts as well as suggestions for improving unsatisfactory conditions.

Resistance and rejection from the school give rise to frequent complaints from parents of gifted children. The highly vocal child advocate is resented and rebuffed in many instances and, while neither side will listen to the other, the child's world suffers. Gifted children offer an unacknowledged threat to insecure teachers. Gifted parents can be quite threatening to school staff as well. In the interests of our children, and with the most to lose or gain, parents should take the initiative in forestalling friction and modelling the prosocial behaviors they hope to elicit in the school staff.

As the gifted child moves into the elementary grades, parents' most frequently reported complaint from their youngsters (both achieving and underachieving) is that "it's boring!" Parents are rightly concerned that a too-easy, unstimulating, overly repetitive curriculum will shape poor work habits, deficient study skills, and

a cavalier attitude toward classroom learning. We know how crucial those early years are in forming school attitudes and situa-
tional self-concepts which have a lasting influence on the child's
progress through school (Whitmore 1980). Those early complaints
about boredom thus merit serious attention and parents should
examine the class work assignments, opportunities for differentiation and challenge. However, it also should be noted that gifted
pupils learn quickly to use "It's boring" as an excuse for not doing
tasks that they simply dislike or, sometimes, that they find too
difficult. The continued use of such an excuse and parental absolu-
tion from the task can result in inadequate foundations in basic
skills or, in some cases, mask a learning disability. Besides, how
many daily necessities do adults also find boring but functional for
work productivity or family well-being. It should be sadly noted
here that children of average and lower abilities report boredom in
school with the same frequency as gifted pupils. This is not an area
in which gifted children are unique.

If it is determined that the school task, even if low in interest,
is a task worth doing, then the gifted child can be helped to get
beyond the tedium in several ways. An explanation of how the
small task fits into a larger whole is helpful; a balance with high
interest activity when the undesirable work is completed; and
importantly the example of the parent doing "boring" but necessary tasks at the same time. Clean the stove while the child does
routine homework at the kitchen table. Sew on buttons or fix a
frayed electrical cord while the assigned worksheets are completed. One parent remarked to me about the distorted perception
today's children must get of their parents' activities. They almost
never actually see their fathers or mothers working. Nearly all
adult work is done either away from the home, or while children
are in school. In the child's eye, parents eat, watch television, read,
and maybe putter a little in the yard. Perhaps mothers and fathers
should consciously save some meaningful parts of their work to do
in company with the child's work, to be followed by a shared
activity that is fun for everyone.

One interesting alternative practice that some parents have
carried out successfully (with the explicit or tacit approval of
school authorities) is the Independent Project Day. One day each
week, usually Wednesday, the gifted child and either parent plan
and carry out learning experiences of the child's choice which are
worthwhile and a motivating reinforcement for conforming to

school requirements on the other four days. Sometimes a simple contract is written, sometimes some product is developed for teacher edification. Such required evidence of work and learning helps to underscore for the child the responsibility of the classroom teacher for validating and recording the child's learning growth.

In working with gifted children whose sensitivity and logical thinking are so deep, teachers and parents often find that a long-respected maxim can be a two-edged sword. Intrinsic motivation, *learning for its own sake*, is a goal to which much lip-service has been paid over the years. The gifted second-grade pupil takes us at our words and says, "I have learned it [or read it, or figured it out] and I know I know it, so why do I have to do this dumb worksheet [write this report, make this project]?" The fourth-grade teacher says, "He understands the social studies material so well and has such interesting ideas about it that he could teach the class if I would let him—but he won't turn in any written work." What a paradox for teacher and pupil! How does the teacher or parent get the child to accept the condition in which we tell her we want her to learn for the sake of learning and for her own satisfaction and, on the other hand, insist that she now demonstrate that learning to the satisfaction of another in ways that she may find redundant or unpleasant. My only solution has been to help the child to understand the teacher's responsibility in certifying the intellectual growth of each pupil and the resulting need for some objective evidence of that growth. If teachers can be fairly flexible in the form that evidence takes, encouraging gifted pupils to share in the design of evaluation strategies, then this approach is usually successful.

For parents there is always the challenge of seeking an appropriate balance in their attitudes toward the gifted child's school performance. They should avoid, at the one extreme, a permissive response to irresponsible work habits and consistent underachievement and on the other extreme, pressure to get As in everything they do.

One common problem reported by youngsters who have been identified by the schools as "gifted" is that teachers seem to think that if they *can* get all "As" then they *should* and parents think they *must.* The child's interests and priorities are often overlooked. As adults, we usually decide that some few things are worth our all-out effort, some others merit medium energy outputs, and a few are done simply at the lowest level of involvement needed for a passable job—and sometimes we decide that something is not worth doing at all when compared to other things which are of more personal value to us. Could we permit our gifted children a modicum of this personal priority setting in deciding which areas merit "A" level energy involvement and which are less interesting or important? Many parents respond to this question with concern about college entrance and the necessity for an outstanding record in order to earn needed scholarships. This is a legitimate concern and one which should be earnestly discussed with the gifted youngster in the framework of the earlier-mentioned creative conformity and the desire for keeping all the options open. However, if this approach does not seem to be productive, avoid continuing pressure and nagging. A child with ability will make her way to college if and when she is ready to go and will be able to enter even if she dropped out of high school and obtained a Graduate Equivalency Diploma. Ivy League colleges and Stanford are not the only places to obtain degrees, and the career paths of gifted and talented youngsters are notably diverse.

One glaring example of parental overanxiety about college preparation surfaced during one of my many talks to parent groups. A mother rose to express concern over her daughter's lack of conscientiousness in preparing homework papers, her haste, lack of neatness, and numerous careless errors even when she knew the material well. Wouldn't this cause a problem for acceptance into college? I replied that good work habits were sometimes a problem for gifted youngsters and asked the mother what grade her daughter was in. "Second grade," she replied. I could not disguise my surprise and disapproval. There are so many more vital things to a seven-year-old than college entrance! One very bright youngster, rebelling against parental and teacher pressures, deliberately earned "Fs" in every sixth-grade subject. When parents put excessive emphasis on grades and communicate, perhaps unwittingly, to a child that school grades are what they care about most, then they put a powerful tool for retaliation in the hands of that child.

Moderation then should be the goal for parents in showing a reasonable concern for productive work and study habits while avoiding unreasonable pressures for across-the-board excellence in achievement at all times.

A related area in which parents should observe moderation is in their reactions to negative teacher conferences. Most parents naturally feel a great deal of identification with their children and usually take personally any criticism of their child. When a teacher complains about a child's achievement or behavior, the parent feels attacked, resentful, responsible, and guilty. This is often followed by anger about experiencing these feelings, and upon whom will this anger be vented? Most frequently the child; the child becomes the scapegoat for the parents' bad feelings. It is true that the teacher has reported her perceptions of the problem but the child has some perceptions of his own, and the reality of the situation probably lies somewhere between. Trying to explore the problem together, without rancor, will be much more likely to bring about desired change than coming home and exploding. Think of it as modelling the kind of problem-solving strategies that you would want the youngster to acquire for use in future crises.

Turning away from discussion of parental reactions to school situations, I would like to offer several proactive roles that parents of gifted youngsters can assume in their interaction with the schools. These are drawn from a 1981 article by Jack Cassidy.

The first role described is *Advisor/Advocate*, in which the parent plays an active part in planning the child's educational program. Help is provided to teachers in identifying the youngster's interests, preferred learning styles, and previous accomplishments, as well as involvement in out of school lessons and hobbies. In addition to assistance in planning, the articulate parent of the gifted should also become an advocate for special programming in the school, publicizing what has been accomplished and gaining support for program expansion. This is a minimal level of involvement and one which schools should encourage and welcome.

A second role is that of *Guide*, enhancing the opportunities provided in the school by activities in the home and by family or group excursions (commonly known as field trips). There are currently a number of publications (see Reference List) offering suggestions for such enrichment and teachers generally urge parents to provide this kind of extra stimulation and exposure for their children. This role requires a larger time commitment from parents but it is usually every enjoyable time. It is often the plan adopted in those cases where parents are keeping their highly gifted children out of the building one day a week to provide variety and challenge that cannot be managed within the traditional framework of the classroom. Many schools see this as a desirable practice.

A third role is that of *Mentor,* harking back to the time-honored apprenticeship model. Many parents of able children have unique skills and talents trained to a very high level. Sometimes their own children do not seem especially interested in the parents' profession, but a gifted schoolmate may desire hungrily the guidance, experience, and inspiration such an adult could provide. Our experience shows the mentor/apprentice relationship to be every bit as rewarding for the adult as for the child. It is a genuine pleasure to share your favorite ideas and skills with a talented and eager learner. In some cases the mentor may serve a group rather than a single individual, as in teaching a foreign language to primary grade children or leading a group in dance or arts activities.

The mentor role is one demanding a significant amount of time and commitment but one which is a two-way street in enjoyment and productivity. The importance of modelling and, if possible, same-sex models, should be stressed when schools encourage parents to take on these responsibilities.

A fourth role, which is also one requiring extensive time commitment, is that of *Classroom Resource Assistant.* This involves providing some special expertise in the classroom by responding to student questions and providing individualized supervision of pupils working on special projects. This provides more in-school flexibility than a single classroom teacher can provide and keeps these high-energy youngsters out of possible mischief under the care of a concerned and interested adult. When parents demand more flexibility and differentiation of instruction from a financially hard-pressed school system, then both male and female parents should consider ways in which they can contribute personally to that effort and this role of Classroom Assistant is an important function.

The fifth role sometimes grows out of the previously described roles and is one which may be more appropriate for a parent not available during school hours. That is the role of *Materials Developer.* There is a tremendous need in gifted education for special curriculum materials to support enrichment or alternative programs.

Although a fair amount of commercial material is currently

becoming available, some of it is not well designed and all of it is expensive. Teacher ideas for Learning Centers or Special Projects can be shared with parents who often have special access to needed materials and/or special talents in the production of needed software or even equipment. Here again is the valuable element of time which the classroom teacher responsible for the instruction of the large group can seldom devote to the unique needs of the few.

When parents are involved in such positive ways with the school, educational difficulties for their children are less likely to develop and, if they do, are more likely to be dealt with in a positive way. Everybody wins!

14

Parent Groups with Shared Concerns

I N THE preceding chapter several ways in which individual parents can work productively with the school were described. Many Parents of the Gifted groups are formed under school auspices, but their activities and benefits go far beyond the school setting. It is true that parents in groups can have a very powerful impact on the schools in ways perceived both positively and negatively by the schools. When parent groups work for the passage of the levy, sponsor various fund raising activities, take responsibility for after-school or weekend enrichment programs, school administrators are happy. When parents seek more flexible programming, hiring of teachers specifically trained to challenge gifted youngsters, and differentiated curriculum, school administrators are usually not quite so pleased. Of course, there are welcome exceptions and their number is happily growing. An example of negative attitude is shown in one suburban school district where teachers are forbidden to suggest to parents of their gifted pupils that they form a support group. Local administrators apparently fear that the disadvantages of group pressure will outweigh the advantages of problem-sharing. Other systems refuse to permit use of the descriptor "gifted," thus effectively preventing any parent groups from emerging. Somehow, "Parents of Able Learners" lack drawing power—and does not really represent the domain of giftedness in its many dimensions.

Although I strongly recommend cooperative, non-adversarial approaches to parent-school interaction, I cannot forget that handicapped children were not served until strong parent groups were formed and pressure was brought to bear on schools and, indispensably, on legislators to bring about improved education for the handicapped. They are a minority, just as the gifted are a minority, but the general attitude in America is much more sympathetic to the less able. When you ask a teacher how much extra time he or she spends in preparation and remediation with the lowest 10 percent of the class and suggest that simple justice would seem to indicate an equal amount of extra time spent in preparation and challenge for the highest 10 percent, the response is one of surprise, followed by resentment. After all, how much can a teacher be expected to do? And so, pragmatically, the higher-ability pupils frequently receive little attention to different needs— "after all," too many teachers say, "they'll get it by themselves— they don't need me; these slow children do. Besides, the law says we must design special programs for the handicapped and I have no time left after that."

That kind of history in special education highlights the importance of parent groups for influencing the lawmakers of local, state, and national legislative bodies. National and state associations for the gifted often sponsor lobbyists in state and national capitols. When funds to support education are limited, as they usually are, we sadly find divisive competition arising between parent groups over support of special programs, with the parents of educationally handicapped in one camp resisting the demands of parents of the gifted who increasingly ask for similar and equitable consideration of special needs. Ideally, all parents groups could come together in support of flexible differentiated instruction in a diagnostic-prescriptive model, but the present funding system based on categorical funding and labelled children makes that goal difficult to achieve. This is one of the major concerns that parent groups should focus on. Often these groups have as members articulate, creative, even powerful people who could take leadership in a cooperative coalition to reduce counterproductive separatism among parent and professional groups. As the parent of a first-born Downs Syndrome daughter and a later-born gifted son exclaimed, "After all we went through with Molly, I never thought we would have to go through the same things with Mark!" Parents who have in one family children at opposite ends of the ability spectrum remark on the many parallels in their interactions with schools in either case. They know first hand that there are grounds for common cause in the demand that all children be appropriately educated.

Even though the majority of parent groups are school based and education is the big priority, there are other desirable functions for such groups.

I have already mentioned problem-sharing or, better, experience sharing. Gifted children themselves often report feeling weird, queer, alone—the only person who is the way he or she is. It is understandable then that many parents feel also that their child is weird, different, the only one like that. Group discussions of the nature and needs of their gifted youngsters and identification of many communalities in their uniqueness can be enlightening and a source of relief and strength for parents struggling to understand their highly gifted offspring. This kind of exploration and exchange generates an awareness of a set of relatively normal traits and behaviors in gifted children. Many of these to-be-expected aspects of giftedness have been extensively described in earlier chapters and I have experienced the relief of parents at group sessions as they recognize the commonality of these traits and begin to overcome that sense that their child is a one-of-a-kind weirdo. Of course this is very helpful for the child as the parent brings a deepened understanding and a heightened confidence to the challenges of child rearing.

One of the advantages of this kind of group discussion is the opportunity for parents to share problem-solutions that have been effective in their families. Of course each child is an individual and no two families are exactly alike, but there are so many shared qualities in the family constellation that such interparent support can be most helpful. An earlier chapter discussed productive responses to problem behaviors and special vulnerabilities. Individual parents can often give specific examples of such responses which have even greater relevance than my necessarily general suggestions.

This setting is also a good one for sharing joys in family experiences. Here, among peers, it should be natural and comfortable to express pleasure and satisfaction in the accomplishments of developing children. Perhaps there is a parallel here to the need for bright children to regularly be grouped with gifted peers to flex their talents and experience similar interests and attitudes in others. One of the things parents do with great enjoyment is talk about their children, and they shouldn't be perennially inhibited by the widespread social unacceptability of excellence in any field but athletics. In a group of parents of the gifted they can more readily share their delight as well as their uncertainty in the unfolding of a child's beauty.

To any parent, counselor, or educator who is thinking of organizing a parent group, let me strongly advise a high priority on group interaction. There are a number of kits available from state and national organizations for those who wish to start a group. They have excellent suggestions for speakers and activities. In my experience with such groups, I find that meeting times are necessarily brief and there is seldom if ever enough time for parents to really get acquainted, develop trust, recognize mutualities, and talk about things with each other. For some meetings, seek out group facilitators rather than expert lecturers—maybe alternately—and strive to develop a genuine support group in a psychological as well as political sense. Many regular school counselors are specially trained in group facilitation and would welcome an opportunity to interact with parents.

Some parent groups have begun library collections for members and their children; in some cases setting up the collection in the local library for use by the community. It is very expensive for one family to purchase all of the informational and recreational reading and media material which is now available in the areas of giftedness and creativity. A library collection with a reserve list is one way of making a wide range of resources available and perhaps raising the consciousness level of the local community. Such a collection would be a boon to teachers, also, as schools have limited budgets for specialized materials and individual salaries rarely permit the accumulation of an extensive professional library. Some publications in the area of giftedness permit single-copy duplication of articles for parent or teacher use, as long as appropriate attribution is given.

Some groups generate a newsletter and regular reviews of materials given to the collection could well appear there. It would be extremely helpful to have gifted youngsters themselves review the books and provide personal reactions to the various selections. Not all of them are first-rate.

Another very important venture for parents groups is the organization of activities for their children. These should include picnics, field trips, sports activities, and cultural events. Gifted youngsters need opportunities to interact informally with gifted peers in other than academic settings. Social graces are often lacking in gifted youngsters because of the frequent awkwardness or rejection experienced in age-peer groups of more average ability. With youngsters more like themselves they can experience more freely the give and take and self-testing that social groups necessarily provide. A child's friends are essential to her development and it is vital that at least some of their number be at the same developmental levels in both cognitive and social competencies and interests.

As a part of this chapter on parent groups, and despite my intent to emphasize all the positive aspects of the parenting of gifted children, I must give attention to some unsettling evidence gathered here and in England (Freeman 1979).

The first bit of data of concern is that the gifted children of parents who join these groups have more academic and personal problems than the similarly gifted children of parents who do not belong to such groups. Freeman (1979) asks, "Do parents join because their children have problems and they seek assistance—or are the parents who join of a type which causes problems for their children?" Certainly more research needs to be done in this area and, within parent groups, more emphasis should be placed on the joys than on the tribulations.

The second disturbing finding is that twice as many parents of boys attend parent groups as do parents of girls, even though the identified school population is almost always fifty-fifty. One emerging factor in the lopsided representation can be discovered in the kinds of responses parents of boys or of girls give to the questions, "How does it feel to be the parent of a gifted child?" and "What was your reaction to the identification of your child as 'gifted'?"

I reported early in this book concerning the most common response we receive to these questions when we survey parents; they most often describe their feelings as "frustrated" or "challenged". The reaction to identification is often to become more insistent that the child perform up to potential.

As I reviewed my data in an effort to develop some hypotheses about the two-to-one ratio of boys' parents to girls' parents in group membership, I decided to tabulate the responses from the two groups separately; in a group of 67 responses representing a number of school systems I found striking and, to me, shocking differences in the kinds of responses given.

To the question, "How do you feel about raising a gifted child?" it was clear that the most frequently occurring responses of "challenging" and/or "frustrating" were given overwhelmingly by the parents of boys. More than 40 percent said this about raising gifted sons, and only 5 percent said this about raising similarly gifted daughters. The most frequent response about rearing gifted daughters was "wonderful," "positive," "fun," with 50 percent answers in that category, while only 21 percent of the parents of sons made that kind of response. Another interesting contrast was related to the response, "It's nothing unusual." While 26 percent of parents of daughters gave this answer, no parents of sons responded in such fashion.

An additional item on which wide sex differences appeared was the question, "What have you told your child about being gifted?" While 30 percent of parents of females responded "nothing," only 10 percent of parents of males made that response, and two of their sons were preschoolers. Another frequent category of response to this item was that the child had a special obligation to use these gifts for the greater good; 22 percent of girls' parents told the child this but only 10 percent of boys' parents gave this service-oriented response. Boys' parents most frequently told them that they could learn more easily than others and they should be thankful for it (18 percent), or that different people have different talents and they should avoid bragging (16 percent).

It is apparent from surveying these 67 parents who are members of school-based parent groups that child-rearing attitudes and concerns indicate worrisome sex-related differences. Parents are much more concerned about providing appropriate experiences and opportunities for boys than girls. The mere fact that boys' parents in these organizations outnumber girls' parents 2 to 1 is disheartening. The substantial differences in the way parents respond to males and females, while it shows much less parental concern about the daughters' development, may also be a blessing in disguise in that it sometimes puts less parental pressure on the girls. Those parents of girls who saw childrearing as a challenge also saw it positively; most parents of boys who reported the task as challenging also found it frustrating. This does not bode well for parent-son relationships and seems to reflect a high degree of parent anxiety about a boy's productivity which will surely be transmitted to the child.

Thus, one of the goals I stress for parent groups is to see the very real challenge of raising gifted children as a positive, reward-ing experience which far outweighs the occasional frustrations. The group members can be mutually supportive in strengthening this attitude. They should also give major focus to the primary role of the family in nurturing the self-concept of the child. Then they can contribute their shared strength to the support of effective educational programming in their schools and the development of enriching extracurricular activities that provide shared social in-teractions in non-academic settings for their gifted offspring. On the wider scene, they can make a significant contribution to state and federal legislation that broadens the educational opportunities for gifted and talented children. All of these efforts should attract equally the parents of girls and of boys.

15

Community Resources

O FTEN, local schools are unable to make adequate provision for the educational challenge of highly gifted learners. Frequently I find that they are not unwilling but generally untrained in this specialized area and nearly always financially pinched. Thus, although fairness would demand equity in education adaptations at both the top and the bottom of the ability spectrum, the legal mandate for services to the lower ability child leaves most school systems with limited resources to devote to individualized services for the highest ability pupils.

Thus, the parents of gifted children will always be primary figures in the education of their exceptionally bright youngsters. It is hoped that they will relish the opportunity to share in the child's blossoming capabilities and joyfully give some priority in the family schedule to challenge opportunities. Such an attitude is so much more productive for both parents and children than anger and frustration with a school staff underprepared and underfinanced.

Wise parents of gifted youngsters begin early to explore the area for community resources for enrichment activities. They make fruitful use of zoos, libraries, and museums of all kinds, historical, science, health, art, botanical gardens, arboretums, which usually offer special classes and also volunteer work opportunities for children who show early interest and talent in specialized areas. Libraries and museums also host meetings for groups like Sierra Club, Gem and Mineral Societies, Great Books groups, Photography clubs, art and music groups or stamp and coin collectors, birdwatchers, herpetologists, butterfly netters, garden enthusiasts, etc. These groups welcome young members and gladly share their experiences and skills with a prospective devotee. Such opportunities are more numerous in urban settings but smaller towns and rural areas will have a few. Travels to the nearest big city or park nature center on a weekly basis may be a valuable investment in a child's present and future use of time and talents.

Local industries or research labs as well as nature preserves should also be investigated if a child expresses a particular technological interest. For political reasons, the federal government has scattered its research and development centers throughout the country and they usually have budgets and staff designated for education and public relations functions. Not only do they host tours and offer special programs but they may also serve as the source of a personal mentor for a bright apprentice. Talented adults are often quite enthusiastic about entering into planned mentoring relationships with highly able children who have special interests in their areas of expertise (Mattson 1983). It is satisfying and rewarding to find a receptive audience for your most valued and hard-won knowledge and skill and to find comprehension and a similar curiosity in a fertile young mind. Life-long friendships have resulted from such early associations and sometimes the special interest continues as an avocation if not an adult career. It is advantageous for parents to learn what sorts of nontraditional careers are possible for youngsters with special interests in nature or the arts. There are many professions other than doctor, lawyer, engineer. Exploring the life styles and educational preparation of experts in diverse fields can be a fascinating and eye-opening pursuit for the whole family. It would certainly go far beyond the ubiquitous Career Day at the high school. Cataloging and describing area resources is an excellent community service which a parent group can maintain.

One of the things we know about gifted children and careers is that these youngsters have multiple talents and multiple interests. It is very difficult for them to select a single path and close out other attractive options. Early, in-depth, experiences in interest areas can help a youngster to look at both vocation and avocation, work and leisure-time activities and may promote exciting and novel combinations. Librarians, curators, docents, tour guides can be gold mines of information and expertise.

Parent groups are themselves community resources and they can also be a source of mentorships or the sponsor of special activities for gifted youngsters. Think how much more exciting and expanding it would be for a group of parents to pool their funds and hire a French or Spanish or Japanese (or any other language) teacher to work with a group of preschoolers than to urge them precociously into school books or computer programs. Language learning activities are so intensely developmentally right for preschoolers that it seems a shame not to take advantage of the special plasticity and elasticity of the language centers of the brain at this time. In small school systems where there are few gifted children at a given age level, some parent groups have joined with similar groups in neighboring school systems to form regional networks and share special programs and resources.

Avoid being sexist about participation in a wide variety of activities. It should go without saying that girls may be just as interested in the Space Center or the Antique Car Museum as their brothers are and that boys can find oral history or counted cross-stitch designing just as engrossing as their sisters do.

One of the more challenging aspects of the search for suitable mentors in the community has been that of locating same-sex role models in careers for women. Making these pairings has proved deeply gratifying for both the mature and the young partner and well worth the efforts of the matchmaker counselors.

Parents of gifted children often have high levels of expertise in their own careers or hobbies. They should not overlook themselves as mentoring resources outside the immediate family circle. If you sail, bicycle, make models, collect political paraphernalia, operate a ham radio, or any of a host of individual pursuits, you may be able to open new doors to inquiring minds and exploring eyes and hands.

One other use of community resources which should be mentioned here is related to Renzulli's Enrichment Triad (1976) and the desirability of finding a genuine and productive outlet or audience for the projects on which gifted youngsters embark. These may originate in school or out of school so it behooves parents to become as aware as possible of community agencies, institutions, and enterprises and points of leverage to which involved youngsters can address the products of their research and creative activity.

Parents can help ultimately in leading the community to see

its gifted children as a valuable resource with genuine contributions to make to the quality of life. As long as our able young people believe that they can change the world and continue to strive to make it a better home for all peoples, there is hope for the planet's future. We weaken that belief and stifle their striving at the peril of humanity.

16

Letting Go

PARENTING in the American culture is a truly ambivalent task. We genuinely want our youngsters to become self-sufficient, productive adults. We also want them to remain closely tied to us as sons and daughters. Our minds want them to become strong and independent but our hearts are reluctant to set them free. Parents of gifted children are sometimes unwilling to encourage career interests or life styles which may pull the maturing son or daughter far from the family orbit.

This tug-of-war in parenting often begins earlier in the families of gifted children than in most families. The gifted youngster shows signs at nine or ten of wanting to take more control of her own life. There are demands for private space, both physical and psychological. There is insistence on a more significant role in family decision-making as it may affect that child. The pre-adolescent may question and test parental value systems in ways traditionally associated with the teen-age years. Parents look back wistfully to the relative calm of early childhood when getting up at night was the biggest burden. Now they look ahead with trepidation to waiting up at night and the burden of setting appropriate limits.

The challenge for parents in these years of transition from childhood to young adulthood is to respond honestly to the maturing intellect and rationality of the child while maintaining a firm hand in encouraging age-appropriate social activities. Knowledge is not wisdom and precocity seldom nurtures prudence. Where parental judgments relative to physical and psychological safety conflict with the wishes of the child, the parent must prevail in the best interests of the youngster. Such conflicts often arise because of the tendency of gifted children to make friends with youngsters older than themselves who may have access to the family car or be already dating. High intellectual ability does not equip the gifted youngster for early entry into the rites of adolescence.

That being understood, there are other areas of maturation in which it may be appropriate to give problem-solving and decision-making opportunities and responsibilities to a gifted youngster earlier than his age-peers are ready to take them on.

Some examples of ways in which we can demonstrate to our youngsters our respect for and trust in their emerging maturity are in the area of self-regulation. To what extent do you permit your son or daughter to have genuine freedom of choice? In the clothing they wear, the schedule of daily activities, the arrangement and decoration of some part of the home, personal budget. One nine-year-old girl who was wearing her mother to a frazzle with her constant need to have the last word in every dialogue with her parents was expressing her need for more autonomy in the only way she found possible. Providing her with some of the freedoms suggested above, beginning with control of her own homework time and gradually increasing her self-management options, significantly reduced what her parents had perceived as rudeness alone. Rude it was, but understanding of the root cause of problem behaviors allows the parent to provide productive alternatives instead of destructive confrontation while it reduces the tension level in the home.

Rising to the challenges of identifying productive alternatives, and risking them, is much healthier for all than the venting of frustration and anger in fruitless controversy. Regular application in the family of creative problem solving activities is a rewarding investment of time and energy.

Of course, part of this letting go involves a determination to avoid sheltering the child from the outcomes of her choices and decisions. This seems to be very difficult to carry through and so we take back a little of the freedom we had offered when we do not allow the freedom to learn from mistakes, to cope with disappointment, to respond to occasional failures. If we want our gifted children to acquire prudence and wisdom in some degree proportionate to their advanced mental abilities, then we must carefully and lovingly let them try out their autonomy and, as much as possible, live with the consequences of their decisions.

Earlier chapters have discussed the difficulties parents experience in refraining from pressuring their children to follow the dreams that they themselves have held or to pursue the career goals which are so attractive to the parents. There is in this an element of self-projection and vicarious gratification that should be eliminated as far as possible. Parental pride is a rewarding feeling and usually very gratifying to the child but if it is too selective in its focus and over-emphasized in a child's reinforcement system, it can have negative effects on a youngster's concept of self as a whole and individual person. The child who deliberately fails in an area which parents have given obvious priority in their own values and reward system is making a desperate request to his parents to see and respond to other aspects of his being than the one in which they seem to take the most pride. Let go of your own priorities to the extent that you can show pleasure in the things that are of priority to the child. Let go of your preconceptions of what you want for the child in order to open yourself to see what the child wants for himself. The nuclear physicist Frederick Dyson's story of his relationship with his son, as described in *The Starship and The Canoe* (Brower 1978) is rich with insights in this regard.

When she shows signs of wanting to try her own wings, have faith enough to let her and honesty enough to recognize that sometimes her choices for herself are as valid as yours may be.

Having young children, nurturing them, and feeling needed is a naturally enjoyable major aspect of every parent's life. It is painful to realize that one is becoming less needed and so one is ambivalent in the pleasure at seeing the devotion to those early child-rearing years bearing fruit in a growing self-sufficiency and a need for separation from parental guidance and support.

One of the most valuable parts of a booklet that Felice Kaufmann (1976) prepared for parents is the section containing suggestions which other parents have found helpful in raising their gifted children. I would like to close this chapter with one of them.

> My suggestion is to try to understand that your gifted child is one who sees things differently. Find out what those ways are. Accept him for what he is and refer often to Khalil Gibran:

"Your children are not your children but the sons and daughters of life's longing for itself. You may give them your love but
not your thoughts. You may house their bodies but not their
souls, for their souls dwell in the house of tomorrow which you
cannot visit, not even in your dreams. And though they are
with you, they belong not to you."

They belong, as each of us does, to themselves. The gifted
individual's most valuable contribution to the good of society is in
simply being all that he or she can be. We are all richer for that.

References

Altman, R. (1983). Social-emotional development of gifted children and adolescents: A research model. *Roeper Review, 6*(2), 65–68.

Applegate, T., & Evans, K. (1985). *Making rational decisions.* Salt Lake City, Utah: RDM CATS, National Diffusion Network.

Baldwin, A. Y., Gear, G. H., & Lucito, L. J. (1978). *Educational planning for the gifted.* Council for Exceptional Children: Reston, VA.

———. (1983). Gender schema theory and its implications for child development: raising gender-aschematic children in a gender-schematic society. *Signs, 8*(4), 598–616.

Bem, S. L. (1973). On liberating the female student. *School* Psychology Digest, 2 (3), 10–18.

Bentzen, C. (1979). The brightest kids. *Saturday Review, 12*(25), 36–40 and cover.

Betts, G. T., & Neihart, M. F. (1985). Eight effective activities to enhance the emotional and social development of the gifted and talented. *Roeper Review, 8*(1), 18–23.

Bloom, B. S. (1985). *Developing talent in young people.* New York: Ballentine Books.

———. (1982). The role of gifts and markers in the development of talent. *Exceptional Children, 48*(6), 510–22.

———. (1964). *Stability and change in human characteristics.* New York: Wiley.

——— & Sosniak, L. (1981). Talent development vs. schooling. *Educational Leadership, 39*(2), 86–94.

Brower, K. (1978). *The starship and the canoe.* New York: Holt, Rinehart & Winston.

Buescher, T. M. (1985). A framework for understanding the social and emotional development of gifted and talented adolescents. *Roeper Review, 8*(1), 10–14.

Cassidy, J. (1981). Parental involvement in gifted programs. *Journal for the Education of the Gifted, 4*(3), 284–287.

Colangelo, N. (1985). Counseling needs of culturally diverse gifted students. *Roeper Review, 8*(1), 30–32.

Coopersmith, S. (1967). *The antecedents of self-esteem.* San Francisco: W. H. Freeman.

Davis, G. A., & Rimm, S. G. (1985). *Education of the gifted and talented.* Englewood Cliffs, N.J.: Prentice-Hall.

DeBono, E. (1971). *Lateral thinking for management: A handbook of creativity.* New York: American Management Association.

———. (1970). *Lateral thinking.* New York: Basic Books.

Dirkes, M. A., (1983). Only the gifted can do it. *Educational Horizons,* 59(3), 138–42.

Domino, G. (1979). Creativity and the home environment. *Gifted Child Quarterly, 24*(4), 818–828.

———. (1969). Maternal personality correlates of son's creativity. *Journal of Consulting and Clinical Psychology, 33,* 180–183.

Drews, E. M. (n.d.). *Creative intellectual style in gifted adolescents, I, II, III.* Michigan: Michigan State University.

Eberle, R., & Stanish, R. (1980). *CPS for kids.* Buffalo, N.Y.: D.O.K. Publishers.

Erikson, E. H. (1963). *Childhood and society* (2nd ed.). New York: W. W. Norton.

Feldhusen, J. F., & Treffinger, D. J. (1977). *Creative thinking and problem-solving in gifted education.* Dubuque, Iowa: Kendall-Hunt.

Feldhusen, J. F., & Wyman, A. R. (1980). Super Saturday: design and implementation of Purdue's special program for gifted children. *Gifted Children Quarterly, 24*(1), 15–21.

Feldman, D. (1979). The mysterious case of extreme giftedness. In A. H. Passow (Ed.), *The gifted and talented: Their education and development,* 78th Yearbook NSSE, Part I. Chicago: University of Chicago Press.

Feldman, R. D., (1982). *Whatever happened to the Quiz Kids?* Chicago, Ill.: Chicago Review Press.

Ferri, E. (1976). *Growing up in a one parent family.* Windsor, Ontario: NFER.

Fleming, E., & Hollinger C., et al. (1979). *Creating her options in career exploration.* Boston: Educational Development Corporation.

Fleming, E., & Takacs, C. (1983) A model for educating teachers of the gifted and talented. *Roeper Review, 6,* 22–26.

Frasier, M. M. (1979). Counseling the culturally diverse gifted. In N. Colangelo & R. T. Zaffrann (Eds.), *New voices in counseling the gifted.* Dubuque, Iowa: Kendall-Hunt, 19–36.

Freeman, J. (1979). *Gifted Children.* Baltimore, MD: University Park Press.

Galbraith, J. (1985). The eight great gripes of gifted kids: responding to special needs. *Roeper Review, 8*(1), 15–17.

Gallagher, J. J. (1985). *Teaching the gifted child.* Boston: Allyn & Bacon.

Gilbreth, F. B. Jr., & Carey, E. G. (1948). *Cheaper by the dozen.* New York: T. Y. Crowell.

Goertzel, V., & Goertzel, M. G. (1962). *Cradles of eminence.* Boston: Little, Brown.

Gowan, J. C. (1983, November). *Creativity as transcendance.* Address delivered at the conference of the National Association for Gifted Children, Philadelphia, PA.

————. (1972). *Development of the creative individual.* San Diego: Knapp.

————, & Torrance, E. P. (1971). *Educating the ablest.* Ithaca, II.: Peacock.

Graham, P. A. (1978). Expansion and exclusion: a history of women in American higher education. *Signs, 3,* 759–773.

Grant, T., & Domino, G. (1976). Masculinity-femininity in fathers of creative male adolescents. *Journal of Genetic Psychology, 129,* 19–27.

Guilford, J. P. (1967). *The nature of human intelligence.* New York: McGraw-Hill.

Hess, R. D., & Shipman, V. C. (1965). Early experience and the socialization of cognitive modes in children, *Child Development, 36*(4), 869–886.

Hise, B. (1979). *A different kind of boy.* Phoenix, AZ: Resources for the Gifted.

Hofstader, R. (1963). *Anti-intellectualism in American Life.* New York: Knopf.

Hollinger, C., (1983). Self-perceptions and the career aspirations of mathematically talented female adolescents. *Journal of Vocational Behavior, 22*(1), 49–62.

Hollingsworth, L. S. (1942). *Children above 180 I. Q..* New York: World.

————. (1927). *Gifted Children.* New York: MacMillan.

Horner, M. (1972). Toward an understanding of achievement related concepts in women. *Journal of Social Issues, 28*(2), 157–175.

Howley, C. B., & Howley, A. A. (1985). A personal record: Is acceleration worth the effort? *Roeper Review, 8*(1), 43–45.

Hunt, J. McV. (1961). *Intelligence and experience.* New York: Ronald Press.

James, W. (1899). Talks to teachers on psychology. In F. Burkhardt (Ed.) (1983), *The works of William James.* Cambridge: Harvard University Press.

Johnson, T. F., & Roth, H. (1985, March/April). Being gifted at home. *G/C/T, 37,* 7–9.

Kaufmann, F. (1976). *Your gifted child and you.* Reston, VA: Council for Exceptional Children.

Kerr, B. A. (1985). Smart girls, gifted women: special guidance concerns. *Roeper Review, 8*(1), 30–32.

Khatena, J., (1982). *Educational psychology of the gifted.* New York: Wiley.

————. (1978). *The creatively gifted child: Suggestions for parents and teachers.* New York: Vantage Press.

Kline, B. E., & Meckstroth, E. A. (1985). Understanding and encouraging the exceptionally gifted child. *Roeper Review, 8*(1), 24–29.

Kohlberg, L. (1969). *Stages in the development of moral thought and action.* New York: Holt, Rinehart & Winston.

Laitin, K., Laitin, S., & Laitin, L. (1978). *The world's #1 best selling soccer book.* Soccer for Americans, Box 836, Manhattan Beach, CA 90266.

Leaverton, L., & Herzog, S. (1979, Spring). Adjustment of the gifted child. *Journal for the Education of the Gifted, 2*(3), 149–152.

Lewis, D. (1979). *How to be a gifted parent: Realize your child's full potential.* New York: Norton.

Lynn, D. B. (1974). *The father: his role in child development.* Monterey, CA: Brooks/Cole.

Marland, S. P., (1972). *Education of the gifted and talented*, Vol. 1. Report to the Congress of the United States by the U.S. Commissioner of Education, Washington, D.C., U.S. Government Printing Office.

Martinson, R. A. (1974). *The identification of the gifted and talented.* Ventura, CA: Office of the Ventura County Superintendent of Schools.

Maslow, A. H. (1954). *Motivation and personality.* New York: Harper & Row.

Mattson, B. (1983). Mentors for the gifted and talents: Whom to seek and where to look. *G/C/T, 27*, 10–11.

McCarthy, R. (1980). Performance anxieties in children: Implications for the young gifted child. In S. Kaplan (Ed.), *Educating the preschool/primary gifted and talented.* Ventura, CA: LTI Publications.

Mead, M. (1939). *Male and female.* New York: Morrow.

Meeker, M. (1978). Extending the definable gifted: Psychic children. In D. M. Jackson (Ed.), *Readings in curriculum development for the gifted.* Guilford, CT: Special Learning Corporation, 100–101.

Moss, H. A. (1967). Sex, age, and state as determinants of mother-infant interaction. *Merrill-Palmer Quarterly, 13*(1), 19–36.

Mussen, P. H. (Ed.). (1970). *Manual of child psychology.* New York: John Wiley & Sons.

Nichols, R. (1964). Parental attitudes of mothers of intelligent adolescents and creativity of their children. *Child Development, 35*, 1041–1049.

Parker, M., & Colangelo, N. (1979). An assessment of values of gifted students and their parents. In N. Colangelo & R. T. Zaffrann (Eds.) *New voices in counseling the gifted.* Dubuque, Iowa: Kendall-Hunt.

Parnes, S. J., Noller, R. B., & Biondi, A. M. (1977). *Guide to creative action.* New York: Scribners.

Passow, H. (1979) *The gifted and talented: Their education and development.* 78th Yearbook NSSE, Part I. Chicago: University of Chicago Press.

Pepinsky, P. (1960). Study of productive nonconformity. *Gifted Child Quarterly, 4*, 81–85.

Perez, G. (1980). Perceptions of the young gifted child. *Roeper Review, 3*(2), 9–11.

Piaget, J. (1962). *Play, dreams and imitation in childhood*. New York: W. W. Norton.

———. (1955). *The language and thought of the child*. New York: World Publishing Company.

———. (1952). *The origins of intelligence in children*. New York: International Universities Press.

Renzulli, J. S. (1976). The enrichment triad model: A guide for developing defensible programs for the gifted and talented. *Gifted Child Quarterly, 20*, 303–326.

Rowlands, P. (1974). *Gifted children and their problems*. London: J. M. Dent.

Schaffer, M. (1980). Child development principles and the gifted preschooler. *Roeper Review, 3*(2), 7–9.

Schwartz, L. L. (1980). Advocacy for the neglected gifted: Females. *Gifted Child Quarterly, 24*, 113–117.

Strang, R. (1960). *Helping your gifted child*. New York: E. P. Dutton.

Takacs, C. (1982) They don't get gifted until fourth grade: what parents can do until then. *Roeper Review, 4*, 43–45.

Terman, L. (Ed.) (1925). *Genetic studies of genius*. (Vol. I). California: Stanford University Press.

———, & Miles, C. C. (1936). *Sex and personality: studies in masculinity and feminity*. New York: McGraw-Hill.

Torrance, E. P. (1979). *The search for satori and creativity*. Great Neck, New York: Creative Synergetic Associates.

———. (1976). Creativity testing in education. *The Creative Child and Adult Quarterly 1*(3), 136–48.

Vail, P. L. (1979). *World of the gifted child*. New York: Penguin Books.

Wallinga, C. R., & Crase, S. J. (1979). Parental influences in the creativity of fifth grade children. *Gifted Child Quarterly, 23*(4), 768–777.

Ward, M. C. (1971). *Them Children*. New York: Holt, Rinehart & Winston.

Weinstein, J. B., & Bobko, P. (1980). The relationship between creativity and androgyny when moderated by an intelligence threshold. *Gifted Child Quarterly, 24*(4), 162–166.

White, B. L. (1971). *Human infants: experience and psychological development*. Englewood Cliffs, NJ: Prentice-Hall.

White, R. W. (1959). Motivation reconsidered: The concept of competence. *Psychology Review, 66*, 297–333.

Whitmore, J. R. (1980). *Giftedness, conflict, and underachievement*. Boston: Allyn and Bacon.

Wilkie, V. (1985). Richardson study, Q-s and A-2 *G/C/T, 36*, 2-9.

Willings, D. (1985). The specific needs of adults who are gifted. *Roeper Review, 8*(1), 35–38.

Resources for Parents of Gifted and Talented Children

PERIODICALS

Gifted Children Monthly
P.O. Box 7200
Bergenfield, NJ 07621
(formerly Gifted Children Newsletter)
Subscription $24 annually
> This publication is primarily for parents and digests important articles published elsewhere, reviews books, and has an excellent section with activities for young people. There is an "Ask the Experts" section and a regular section in which toys, games, computer software, etc., are evaluated. This is a very useful resource which some parent groups donate to the local library for multiple users.

G/C/T
5 P.O. Box 6448
Mobile, AL 36660
Published six times per year, subscription $24.00 annually.
> This magazine is primarily for teachers and parents and is one of the most widely read periodicals in the field. The contributors include gifted youngsters, classroom teachers, as well as nationally recognized experts in giftedness. It contains excellent curriculum examples and a regular section on parenting concerns. (Gifted/Creative/ Talented)

Gifted Child Quarterly
National Association for Gifted Children
5100 North Edgewood Drive
St. Paul, MN 55112

Published quarterly, subscription included in membership in the above
organization (membership fee, $26.00 annually).
This is a scholarly journal with an emphasis on research-based
articles in areas of interest to parents, educators, and psychologists.
It is usually available in libraries and is well worth investigating.

Journal for the Education of the Gifted
Council for Exceptional Children
Reston VA 22091
This journal is a quarterly included with membership in CEC's
division on Gifted and Talented. It also contains scholarly articles as
well as articles on issues of direct concern to parents. Its audience is
mainly teachers and university professionals. It is available in most
academic libraries. This would be a good journal for parent groups
to donate to the professional library of their schools.

Roeper Review
P.O. Box 329
Bloomfield Hills, MI 48013
This is a quarterly published by the Roeper City and Country School
for gifted youngster. Subscription $20.00 annually.
It is an outstanding scholarly journal with a regular section on
parenting and another on educational programs. It includes book
reviews and philosophical articles as well as research on giftedness.
This journal is recommended reading for all who are interested in
gifted children.

BOOKS

Supergrow by Benjamin Mott, 1969.
A witty and most intelligent collection of essays, of which the title
"Supergrow" is a thought-provoking discussion of the highly
publicized efforts to produce super babies. Excellent treatment of
imagination in America.
E.P. Dutton, New York, NY

Raising your Gifted Child by J. V. Flowers, J. Horsman, and B. Schwartz,
1982.
The authors discuss mental health, creativity, and underachievement, and there is a 1982 list of resources and addresses of state and
national associations.
Prentice-Hall, Englewood Cliffs, NJ 07632

Gifted Children: A Guide for Parents and Teachers by V. Z. Ehrlich, 1982.
The author is a long-time director of the Astor Program, a pioneer program in New York City for the early education of gifted children. It contains information on identification and suggests strategies for parent-school interaction and making career decisions.
Prentice-Hall, Englewood Cliffs, NJ 07632

Somewhere to Turn: Strategies for Parents of the Gifted and Talented by E. G. Hall and N. Skinner, 1980.
A small introductory softback with a helpful discussion of the terminology used by professional educators, some interesting case histories, and suggested activities for learning at home.
Teachers College Press, 1234 Amsterdam Avenue, New York, NY 10027

The Creatively Gifted Child: Suggestions for Parents and Teachers by J. Khatena, 1978.
The author discusses the strengths and weakness of the creatively gifted child and gives several suggestions to help support the children, reward him, reduce his anxieties, and encourage him to approach learning as experimentation. This is a positive and most helpful little volume.
Vantage Press, 516 West 34th Street, New York, NY 10001

Your Gifted Child and You by Felice Kaufmann, 1976.
This is a fine, although somewhat dated, publication which contains such material drawn from the author's extensive work with parents. The helpful quotes from parents have been very meaningful for those with whom I have worked.
Council for Exceptional Children, The Association for Gifted Children, 1920 Association Drive, Reston, VA 22091

Mountains to Climb: A Handbook of Resources for the Gifted and Talented by P. A. Haensly and W. R. Nash, 1983.
Contains information about acceleration and enrichment, with suggestions for resources in rural, suburban, and big city environments and special summer programs.
National Association for Gifted Children, St. Paul, MN 55122

Gifted Children by Joan Freeman, 1979.
This worthwhile book treats of the findings and implications of an extensive study of gifted children and their parents in England during the 1970s. It merits thoughtful reading and should give rise to productive introspection.

University Park Press, 233 East Redwood Street, Baltimore, MD
21202

Growing Up Gifted (First Edition) by B. Clark, 1979.
(The revised second edition has taken the possible ramifications of
the new study of the brain too far from the empirical evidence for
my taste.)
The initial volume contained an excellent treatment of the cognitive
and the social and emotional concomitants of growing up as a gifted
child. It contributed a great deal to general understanding of giftedness and also contains good suggestions for educational program
modifications. The book is often used as a textbook for introductory
courses for teachers of the gifted, but parents have also found it
helpful.
Charles E. Merrill, Columbus, OH 43081

NATIONAL ASSOCIATIONS

All of these associations have a special interest in and provide informational materials on parenting gifted and talented youngsters. Most have
annual conferences with special sessions of interest to parents; many also
provide activities for children as part of the conference.

NAGC, The National Association for Gifted Children
5100 N. Edgewood Drive
St. Paul, MN 55112 (612) 784-3475

CEG-TAG, The Council for Exceptional Children
Talented and Gifted Children
1920 Association Drive
Reston, VA 22091 (703) 620-3660

The World Council for the Gifted and Talented
Box 218
Teachers College
Columbia University
New York, NY 10027 (212) 678-3866

The National Leadership Training Institute on the
Gifted and Talented
316 W. Second Street
Suite PH-C
Los Angeles, CA 90012 (213) 489-7470

As of this writing there is no federal Office of the Gifted and Talented; however, nearly every state has a centrally located office for the education of the gifted and talented whose address is available from either your State Department of Education or the governor's office.

Most states also have associations which are branches or spin-offs of the NAGC. Their addresses change with the change of state officers, and headquarters can usually be located through your state educational officer in charge of gifted and talented education.

Local associations are usually affiliated with a school district or a consortium of school districts. Check with your local Coordinator of Gifted Education in district or county or parish for information on parent groups. Many state associations will assist you in organizing a local group of interested parents if none now exists.

CHILDREN'S RESOURCES

The Gifted Kids' Survival Guide by J. Galbraith, 1983.
Wetherall Publishing, 510 First Avenue N., Minneapolis, MN 55403
This book is addressed specifically to teen-age gifted youngsters and responds to their most-often expressed problems. There is also a 1984 publication by the same title which is specifically addressed to elementary school youngsters. Many youngsters find the breezy style attractive and it does help them to understand that other youngsters have the same problems. They may or may not choose the suggested remedies, but they have been effective for the young contributors.

Challenge
Good Apple, Inc.
Box 299, Dept. GCT 15
Carthage, IL 62321-0299
$20.00 annually (5 issues)
Contains activities, projects, and games to stimulate the thinking powers of gifted youngsters aged 4 to 12. Publisher is also a source of good educational materials.

Chart Your Course
P.O. Box 6448
Mobile, AL 3660-0448
$20.00 annually (8 issues)
A magazine by and for creative youngsters, it features games, art, poetry, computer programs, book and movie reviews, musical compositions and journalism produced by gifted contributors. This is an excellent avenue for publication of children's work.

Cricket
Box 100
La Salle, Illinois 61301
Published monthly, subscription $18.50 annually
> This magazine is very attractive to younger gifted children and contains high quality literary material.

The Futurist
World Future Society
4916 St. Elmo Ave.
Bethesda, MD 20814
> An adult magazine with strong appeal to the gifted adolescent. Articles treat trends in technology, life styles, economics, education, government, the future of the planet, relationships to space, etc.

Prism
1040 Bayview Drive, Ste. 223
Fort Lauderdale, Florida 33304
Six issues yearly, subscription $19.95
> This magazine appeals to older children and publishes material submitted by young people.

APPENDIX B

State Offices for Gifted and Talented Education

Alabama
Alabama State Dept. Ed.
868 State Office Bldg.
Montgomery, AL 36130
(205) 261-5099

Alaska
Section for Exceptional
Children
Dept. of Education
Goldbelt Place
810 W. 10th St., Pouch F.
Juneau, AK 99811
(907) 465-2970

American Samoa
Gifted/Talented Education
Pago Pago, AS 96799

Arizona
Div. of Special Education
Arizona Dept. of Education
1535 West Jefferson
Phoeniz, AZ 85007
(602) 255-5008

Arkansas
Programs for G/T
Special Education Section
Arch Ford Education Bldg.
Little Rock, AR 72201
(501) 371-2161

California
G/T Education
721 Capital Mall
Sacramento, CA 95814
(916) 323-4781

Colorado
Colorado Dept. of Ed.
201 East Colax
Denver, CO 80203
(303) 866-5271

Connecticut
State Dept. of Ed.
165 Capitol Ave.
Hartford, CT 06145
(203) 566-3695

Delaware
Programs/Except. Children
Dept. Public Instruction
P.O. Box 1402
Townsend Building
Dover, DE 19903
(302) 736-4667

District of Columbia
G/T Education Program
Seaton Elementary School
10th & Rhode Island Ave.
  NW
Washington, DC 2001
(202) 673-7054

Florida
DOE/Bureau of Education
for Exceptional Children
Knott Building
Tallahasse, FL 32301
(904) 488-1106

Georgia
Dept. of Education
Twin Towers E., Suite 1970
Atlanta, GA 39334
(404) 656-2428

Guam
Dept. of Special Ed.
P.O. Box DE
Agana, GU 96910
911-44-671
Local No. 472-8906

Hawaii
Gifted and Talented
Special Needs Branch
Dept. of Education
3430 Leahi Ave.
Honolulu, HI 96815
(808) 737-2377 or 2166

Idaho
State Dept. of Education
Len B. Jordan Office Bldg.
650 West State
Boise, ID 83720
(208) 344-3940

Illinois
State Dept. of Ed.
100 North First St.
Springfield, IL 62777
(217) 782-3810

Indiana
Gifted/Talented Ed.
Indiana Dept. of Ed.
Room 229 State House
Indianapolis, IN 46204
(317) 927-0111

Iowa
Dept. of Public Instruction
Grimes State Office Bldg.
Des Moines, IA 50319
(515) 281-3198

Kansas
State Dept. of Ed.
120 E. 10th Street
Topeka, KS 66612
(913) 296-3743

Kentucky
Kentucky Dept. of Ed.
1825 Capitol Plaza Tower
Frankfort, KY 40601
(502) 564-2672

Louisiana
State Dept. of Ed.
P.O. Box 44064
Baton Rouge, LA 70804
(504) 342-3636

Maine
   State House Station #23
   Augusta, ME 04333
   (207) 289-3451

Maryland
   State Dept. of Ed.
   200 W. Baltimore St.
   Baltimore, MD 21201
   (301) 659-2363

Massachusetts
   Mass. Dept. of Ed.
   Bureau of Curric. Services
   1385 Hancock St.
   Quincy, MA 02135
   (617) 770-7237

Michigan
   Michigan Dept. of Ed.
   P.O. Box 30008
   Lansing, MI 48909
   (517) 373-3279

Minnesota
   Gifted Education
   State Dept. of Ed.
   641 Capitol Square
   St. Paul, MN 55101
   (612) 296-4972

Mississippi
   State Consultant/Gifted
   State Dept. of Ed.
   P.O. Box 771
   Jackson, MS 39205
   (601) 359-3488 or 3490

Missouri
   Gifted Education Program
   P.O. Box 480
   100 East Capitol
   Jefferson City, MO 65102
   (314) 751-2453

Montana
   Office of Pub. Instruction
   State Capitol
   Helena, MT 59601
   (406) 444-5660

Nebraska
   State Dept. of Ed.
   300 Centennial Mall South
   Lincoln, NE 68509
   (402) 471-2446

Nevada
   Nevada Dept. of Ed.
   400 West King Street
   Carson City, NV 89710
   (702) 885-3140

New Hampshire
   State Dept. of Ed.
   105 London Road
   Concord, NH 03301
   (603) 271-3741

New Jersey
   Dept. of Ed.
   225 West State St.
   CN 500
   Trenton, NJ 08625-0500
   (609) 292-8412

New Mexico
   Div. of Special Ed.
   Education Building
   Santa Fe, NM 87501-2786
   (505) 827-6541

New York
   Gifted Education
   State Education Dept.
   Room 310 EB
   Albany, NY 12234
   (518) 474-5966

North Carolina
Div. of Except. Children
Dept. of Public Instruction
Raleigh, NC 27611
(919) 733-3004

North Dakota
Dept. of Public Instr.
State Capitol
Bismark, ND 58505
(701) 224-2277

Ohio
Division of Special Ed.
933 High Street
Worthington, OH 43085
(614) 466-2650

Oklahoma
State Dept. of Ed.
2500 N. Lincoln Blvd.
Oklahoma City, OK 73105
(405) 521-4287

Oregon
700 Pringle Parkway SE
Salem, OR 97219
(503) 378-3879

Pennsylvania
Bureau of Special Ed.
Dept. of Ed.
333 Market Street
Harrisburg, PA 17126-0333
(717) 783-6913

Puerto Rico
Consultant, Gifted
Office/External Resources
Dept. of Ed.
Hato Rey, PR 99024
(809) 765-1475

Rhode Island
Dept. of Elem./Second. Ed.
22 Hayes St.
Providence, RI 02908
(401) 277-6523

South Carolina
Programs for the Gifted
802 Rutledge Building
1429 Senate Street
Columbia, SC 29201
(803) 758-2652

South Dakota
Special Education Section
Richard F. Kneip Building
700 N. Illinois
Pierre, SD 57501
(605) 773-3678

Tennessee
132-A Cordell Hull Bldg.
Nashville, TN 37219
(615) 741-3659

Texas
Texas Educational Agency
201 East 11th St.
Austin, TX 78701
(512) 834-4451

Trust Territory
Trust Territ. office of Ed.
Office of the High
Commissioner
Saipan, CM 96950
160-671-Saipan 9312, 9428,
or 9319

Utah
State Office of Education
250 E. 5th South
Salt Lake City, UT 84111
(801) 533-5572

Vermont
　　State Dept. of Ed.
　　Montpelier, VT 05602
　　(802) 828-3111 ext. 33

Virgin Islands
　　State Dir. of Special Ed.
　　Dept. of Ed.
　　Box 630, Charlotte Amalie
　　St. Thomas, VI 00801
　　(809) 774-0100

Virginia
　　Division of Special Ed.
　　Virginia Dept. of Ed.
　　P.O. Box 6Q
　　Richmond, VA 23216
　　(804) 225-2070

Washington
　　Old Capitol Bldg.
　　Olympia, WA 98501
　　(206) 753-6733

West Virginia
　　Programs for the Gifted
　　357 B, Capitol Complex
　　Charleston, WV 25305
　　(304) 348-7010

Wisconsin
　　P.O. Box 7841
　　125 S. Webster
　　Madison, WI 53707
　　(608) 266-3560

Wyoming
　　Wyoming Dept. of Ed.
　　Hathaway Bldg.
　　Cheyenne, WY 82002
　　(307) 777-6238

Index

ENJOY YOUR GIFTED CHILD

was composed in 10-point Mergenthaler Linotron 202 Aster and leaded 2 points
by Coghill Book Typesetting Co.,
with display type in Bulletin Typewriter by Rochester Mono/Headliners;
printed sheet-fed offset on 50-pound, acid-free Glatfelter B-31,
Smyth sewn and bound over 80-point binder's boards in Holliston Roxite B,
also adhesive bound with paper covers by Thomson-Shore, Inc.;
with paper covers printed in 2 colors by Thomson-Shore, Inc.;
and published by

SYRACUSE UNIVERSITY PRESS

SYRACUSE, NEW YORK 13244-5160